B2B

MARKETING

B2B

MARKETING

A radically different approach for business-to-business marketers

STEVE MINETT

PhD & Chartered Marketer

FINANCIAL TIMES

Prentice Hall

An imprint of **Pearson Education**

London · New York · San Francisco · Toronto · Sydney
Tokyo · Singapore · Hong Kong · Cape Town · Madrid
Paris · Milan · Munich · Amsterdam

PEARSON EDUCATION LIMITED

Head Office:
Edinburgh Gate
Harlow CM20 2JE
Tel: +44 (0)1279 623623
Fax: +44 (0)1279 431059

London Office:
128 Long Acre
London WC2E 9AN
Tel: +44 (0)20 7447 2000
Fax: +44 (0)20 7240 5771
Website: www.business-minds.com

First published in Great Britain in 2002

© Pearson Education Limited 2002

The right of Steve Minett to be identified as Author
of this Work has been asserted by him in accordance
with the Copyright, Designs and Patents Act 1988.

ISBN 0 273 65425 X

British Library Cataloguing in Publication Data
A CIP catalogue record for this book can be obtained from the British Library.

10 9 8 7 6 5 4 3 2 1

Designed by Claire Brodmann Book Designs, Lichfield, Staffs.
Typeset by Pantek Arts Ltd, Maidstone, Kent.
Printed and bound in Great Britain by Biddles Ltd, Guildford & King's Lynn.

The publishers' policy is to use paper manufactured from sustainable forests.

Contents

7 Case-based communications 172

8 E-business for B2B 196

Foreword

By Thomas R. Martin

Senior Vice President and Director, Corporate Relations ITT Industries, Inc.

ITT Industries is a classic example of a business to business enterprise. Very few of our products are sold directly to consumers. The overwhelming majority of our revenue come from products and services bought by businesses, municipalities, government agencies, and other organizations. Clearly, this "B2B" marketplace thinks differently, acts differently and has a different set of communication expectations when compared to the business to consumer or "B2C" market.

When I first joined ITT Industries in 1996, the company was faced with a serious identity problem. In the 1960s and 1970s, the old ITT had personified the cliché of the conglomerate, acquiring and divesting scores of companies each year in diverse fields, from financial services to forestry; from insurance to hotels, manufacturing, and telecommunications. In December of 1995, the huge company split into three separate organizations: one focussed on insurance, one on gaming and hospitality, and finally ITT Industries, a diversified manufacturing company.

Yet our customers and investors, even our employees were unsure of exactly what we did. In an effort to address this confusion, we launched a comprehensive campaign in 1998 aimed at unifying our many strong product brands under a clarified corporate brand. As part of this effort, we adopted a new tagline, "Engineered for Life" and began to tell our stories through the voice of our engineers. Steve Minett and his company have helped us tell those stories.

In this new book, Minett skillfully explores the unique selling and communications needs of the B2B market. As he explains, organizations are motivated by a particular set of market drivers and a purchasing decision process that is quite different from the consumer market. B2B purchasing decisions are driven more by needs than wants, more by technological applications than changing fashion.

As a result, the B2B marketplace lends itself especially well to the use of case studies, stories of successful applications and end-use solutions made possible by the products or services provided by the selling organization. In many ways, these case stories help spark the imagination of the buyer, presenting a range of new possibilities not always obvious from a simple description of product features.

Steve Minett's ideas aren't just interesting theoretical suppositions; they actually work. On behalf of ITT Industries, Minett Media has, in recent years, placed approximately 350 articles in the international trade press. In terms of the cost of equivalent advertising space, these placements represent a value of around $2 million, while the cost of achieving these results (including the cost of article production) has amounted to less than $150,000, less than 7.5% of the value. More importantly, this editorial coverage leads to actual buyer interest and, ultimately, sales.

Trade publications are eager for material that is of interest to their readers. Minett's approach in telling interesting stories helps to break through the clutter and connect with an audience of interested prospects. It may seem more glamorous to be featured in *Fortune*, *Forbes*, or *Business Week*, but articles in these major media rarely lead to direct sales. Trade coverage, on the other hand, often does.

Minett is clearly on to something. Anyone trying to sell a product or service in the B2B world will benefit from his advice. Businesses are more than a sum total of tangible assets; at heart, organizations represent a collection of imagination, solutions, and ideas. Steve Minett taps into this imaginative world in a novel and creative way. Enjoy his story.

on behalf of ITT Industries, Minett Media has created
a value of $2 million at a cost of $150,000, less than 7.5% of the value

Introduction

Turning experience into a paradigm

This is a book by a practitioner for practitioners. It's based predominantly on experience – using theory only where tested by experience. I've been working as a specialist in B2B marketing communications for almost 20 years. In the early days, I found myself, fairly frequently, turning the following questions over in my mind: "Out of the myriad of things I *could* be doing, what is really *important*?" In other words, where should I *focus* my attention? "What do I really *need to do*?" Hopefully, this was not entirely an idiosyncratic problem: of all the management disciplines, perhaps marketing is most in need of Stephen Covey's rigorous prescriptions regarding proactive prioritizing.[1] Marketers are continually confronted by a mass of issues, many of which are, or can be seen as, urgent – but which are *really important*, whether they're urgent or not? Because of the nature of their tasks, accountants and production managers, for example, have much better-developed mechanisms for determining this than do marketers.

THE LIMITS OF A QUANTITATIVE APPROACH

Having trained and practiced as an academic myself (in political science and organizational behavior), my first reaction was to turn to the literature on marketing. Crudely speaking, this comes in two varieties; the output from academics and "self-help" books aimed at practitioners. I started with the academics, since I was studying for professional examinations (I ended up as a chartered marketer). I didn't really find practical answers to my questions about *what* to say in my communications with the market. The initial, and obvious, problem was that the literature is overwhelmingly B2C focussed, while I was asking B2B questions. A deeper problem may be the nature of social science itself: (perhaps inevitably) its answers are often ambivalent and always (and eternally) qualified by the need for further research. My needs, as a practitioner, however, were – and are – too urgent to be satisfied with this.

The sort of research I was really able to use was the sort I could do myself, every-day, at work. Interestingly, one of the most internationally eminent of marketing academics, Evert Gummesson, Professor of Service Management and Marketing at Stockholm University's Business School, has come to similar conclusions:

> I see the researcher as the number one research instrument. I feel at liberty to use myself and my experience as evidence. This would traditionally be classified as a qualitative approach, or worse, as unscientific ... I do not subscribe to the assumption that words are unreliable and fuzzy and merely preliminaries to numbers, which are precise and uncover the truth. ... The academic praise of the supremacy of quantitative measurement shuts out most of *marketing reality* [my italics]. [2]

Significantly, Gummesson also has extensive experience as a marketing practitioner and I would claim that his remarks above apply particularly to B2B marketing, where macro-level empirical data is often particularly scarce and uncertain.

The practitioner self-help books did occasionally provide practical tips but these were generally tucked away amid a mass of checklist advice, which tended to be banally obvious, impractical or – for me as a B2B specialist – irrelevant. (An exception was the *sales* writer, Neil Rackham, whom we'll meet in Chapter One). What I felt I was missing were *insights* into the B2B marketing and sales process, on which I could base my practice: what I really needed was a B2B marketing *paradigm*. This is what I'm trying to describe in this book. As explained above, I found only fleeting glimpses of it in the marketing literature. The really fruitful source proved to be the intensive discussions I've had with B2B practitioners over the last two decades. These involved buyers, sellers (often together) and marketers from many different business areas and in many different countries. These discussions nearly always concerned a *particular case* – an application case and/or a sales case. (I've been conducting discussions of this sort, in order to produce editorial material.) As I see it, a B2B paradigm was (and is) implicit in the behavior and ground-level thinking of these hundreds of B2B practitioners. My ambition in writing this book is to systematize and clearly articulate this "paradigm-in-practice," in order to make it available, as a suggested guide to best practice, for other B2B practitioners.

WHY A "PARADIGM"?

When Leonardo da Vinci was asked to account for his prodigious production of creative works, he replied, "by making an effort to *see*." As a B2B marketer, how do you *see* your professional world? In other words, what is your professional paradigm? I'd like to suggest that having a clearly articulated paradigm – a particular way of seeing the territory you operate in – can provide you with the most useful tool in your professional skills box. Other tools can be used now and then, in particular situations and for particular projects; this one can be wielded daily and throughout your professional life. My strategy at the beginning of the book is to open a gateway into the B2B paradigm via two basic propositions:

● B2B marketing is different enough from B2C to require a distinct professional paradigm

● The essential element to practice within this B2B paradigm is the adoption of a "case-focus" (as opposed to the consumer-focus which is optimal for B2C marketing).

Chapter One identifies the territory of the B2B paradigm, as defined by two dimensions of a four-box table (see Figure 1.2, page 4); "technological products," "self-expressive products" and "organizational buying," "individual buying." The heartland of B2B lies within the "technology-organizational" box. Chapter Two describes why a "case-based" approach to marketing is likely to be the most effective within this B2B territory.

STRATEGY, BRANDING, MARCOMS AND E-BUSINESS

The rest of the book examines how to apply the distinct B2B, case-based paradigm to the following areas:

● new product strategy (Chapter Three)

● branding (Chapter Four)

● channel management (Chapter Five)

● marketing communications (Chapter Five)

- the predominant role which the editorial channel can play in a case-based approach (Chapter Six)

- strategies for case-based responses to market feed-back (Chapter Seven) and

- B2B and the internet – how pioneering companies are applying the paradigm while transforming themselves into "e-businesses" (Chapter Eight).

CASE EXAMPLES

As mentioned above, I've met many B2B marketers who've been intuitively employing this approach. Some of them appear in the book. It contains nine "maxi-cases," specifically written for the book, about how some B2B companies have actually been practicing case-based marketing, in areas such as strategy, branding, and e-business. These cases describe the practice of major global companies, including ITT Industries, Ericsson, Sandvik Steel, and Alfa Laval, and also look at smaller companies in Sweden, America, and the UK. (Most of the companies which appear in this book are clients of my agency, which specializes in B2B marketing communications. Although based in the UK, the agency's practice is concentrated first, in Sweden and second, in America.)

ILLUSTRATIONS

The book also contains two other forms of illustration, first, 28 "mini-cases." These are shortened versions of actual case stories and features on new technologies which my agency has produced for its clients over the last decade or so. I've tried to insert these, at appropriate places in the text as a means of exemplifying the argument I'm making or the practice I'm describing at that point. The other form of illustration consists of the 32 figures which appear in the book. Most of these started life as slides in a presentation I developed to promote my agency's business: our core product is the production and placement in the international trade press of strategic case stories. My presentation was designed to explain why B2B companies should want to do this. As I travelled around Sweden, America, and the UK giving this presentation (mainly to marketing groups in my client companies, but also to branch meetings of the Chartered Institute of Marketing) I found, over the years, that the explanation reached further and further back into the theory of B2B marketing, until – as someone finally pointed out to me – I had enough ideas and material to write a book on the subject.

THE MORAL AMBIVALENCE OF MARKETING

Finally, by way of introduction, I'd like to acknowledge a desire to inject an ethical dimension into the B2B paradigm I present in this book. The personal background to this is as follows: when I meet people socially and announce, "I'm in marketing," I often detect a certain ambivalence in their response. I suspect that this comes from the "image" of marketers in the mass media – manipulative practitioners of "black arts" – "spin doctors" in both politics and the commercial world. I can empathize with the ambivalent response, because, as a consumer of the mass media, I sometimes feel it myself. I vividly remember listening to a radio report describing how children from low-income families are bullied at school because their parents can't afford the "right" brand of trainers or backpack. During the report, a single mother bitterly blamed "the marketing men" for the torment visited upon her child. I recall comforting myself with the reflection, "I, at least, am not in *that* type of marketing." When I meet with the ambivalent response in person, I may try to explain to my new acquaintance that, "I'm in *B2B*, not *consumer* marketing," but even if they know what this means, it doesn't seem to help much.

ETHICS FOR B2B MARKETING

As an integral part of the B2B paradigm, therefore, I'm proposing an ethical dimension, which I believe is implicit in much of B2B practice. Key to this is the idea that B2B marketing is a crucial part of a much larger societal process, i.e. technological development: by the way in which they present technologies which are ready for commercial application, B2B marketers play a role in which of these get adopted and which don't. Consequently, while misrepresentation and manipulation in consumer marketing may damage individuals, in B2B marketing such behavior can also interfere with an important societal process – a process, moreover, which has a significant, long-term impact on human welfare as a whole. These conceptions lie behind the lawyer analogy which I use in the book. I'm aware that lawyers may not be popularly regarded as the most ethical of professions (a number of my B2B marketing colleagues have been particularly resistant to this comparison). What they do have, however, is a set of rules and conventions which are intended to guide them, irrespective of the particular interests which they may be currently representing. Extending the lawyer analogy, I suggest in the book that the ethics of B2B marketing are also concerned with issues such as the "rules of evidence" and the conduct of "rational discourse."

Finally, formulating a professional paradigm for B2B marketing may seem like an overly ambitious undertaking, but let me re-emphasize that this book has grown out of experience: much of it is concerned with making explicit what is implicit in the practice of the many B2B marketers I've met. I very much hope that the case studies in the book (both "maxi" and "mini") will serve to illustrate this point.

NOTES

1. Covey, S. R. (1989) *The Seven Habits of Highly Effective People.* London: Simon & Schuster.
2. Gummesson, E. (2001) Are current research approaches in marketing leading us astray, *Marketing Theory,* 1(1). See also Gummesson (2000) *Qualitative Methods in Management Research.* Thousand Oaks, CA: Sage Productions Inc.

Acknowledgements

As is clear from the Introduction, I have many people to thank for the production of this book. Among friends and colleagues from the B2B world, I'd like to mention first, Björn von Euler (currently Director of Corporate Communications, ITT Fluid Technology & Specialty Products Group, New Jersey). Björn and I first began working together at the world HQ of ITT Flygt in Stockholm in 1988. He was enormously helpful and supportive in the early days of "case-based" marketing and also nurtured the infant Minett Media during its re-location from Stockholm, Sweden, to Cambridge, England. In the mythology of our agency he is known simply as "The Godfather." Another early stalwart was Göran Wijkmark (formerly President of Nordic Water AB and later of Anglian Water Process Engineering, currently CEO of Kasthall AB). Göran was not only an exemplary client, but also a good friend and confidant while we both went through the process of trying to adjust to the transition from Swedish to British business culture. The third "B2B" friend I want to mention here is a newer one, Tom Martin (Senior Vice-President and Director of Corporate Relations, ITT Industries Inc, New York). Tom both very kindly agreed to write the foreword to this book and contributed a "maxi-case" on the re-branding of ITT Industries for Chapter Four.

Many thanks are also due to the other "maxi-case" contributors who gave generously of their time and energy during the preparation of this book: Haljmar Fries (formerly R & D Director at ITT Flygt, now running his own consultancy, X-Nova), Leif Carlsson (formerly CEO of ITT Flygt, now a consultant), Lars Frisk (Marketing Manager, Submersible Mixers, ITT Flygt, Stockholm), Thomas Anderfelt (Marketing Manager, Ericsson Product Unit Modules, Bilbao, Spain), Enrique Pedrosa Gomez (Key Account Manager, Ericsson Product Unit Modules, Bilbao, Spain), Peter Friedrichsen (CEO, MaxMove AB, Stockholm), Hayes Roth (Vice President Americas Marketing at Landor Associates, New York), Peter Torstensson (Vice President of Corporate Communications, Alfa Laval AB, Lund, Sweden), Bengt Eriksson (Head of Landor Associates' Stockholm office), Göran Nyström (Vice President for Sales & Marketing at Sandvik Steel, Sandviken, Sweden), Annika Roos (Marketing Communications Manager at Sandvik Steel, Sandviken, Sweden), David Povich (President of Tool Alliance, California), Hans

Söderhjelm (Marketing Manager, Höganäs AB, Höganäs, Sweden), Mark Goetze (Director of e-business, ITT Industries Inc, New York).

Thanks for permission to publish the 28 "mini-cases" in the book go to: Lars Stenmark (Development Director, Chematur AB, Karlskoga, Sweden), Göran Eckeström (Export Manager, MaxMove AB, Stockholm), Niclas During (Marketing Communications Manager, Sandvik Hard Materials, Stockholm), Jan Olofsson (Marketing Communications Manager, Svedala AB, Malmö, Sweden), Per Arvedsson (Marketing Communications, GL&V Sweden AB), Agneta Lindquist (Marketing Communications Manager, Kemwater, Kemira Kemi AB, Helsingborg, Sweden), Steve Barstow (Sales & Marketing Manager, Heathline Products Ltd, Amphill, UK), Mikael Byström (Vice President Corporate Relations, Trelleborg AB, Trelleborg, Sweden), Leif Öberg (Vice President Corporate Relations, Boliden, Stockholm), Bo Andersson, (Marketing Communications Manager, Nordic Water Products, Waterlink AB, Nynäshamn, Sweden), Monica Spendilow (Marketing Communications Manager, ITT Flygt, Stockholm), and Martin Lindfors (Marketing Communications, Sandvik Construction & Mining).

In addition to those named above, there have also been several hundred others; sales people and customers of the above companies, plus many other companies, who, during our meetings and discussions, contributed in one way or another to the ideas expressed in this book – to one and all a heart-felt thanks.

One of the great joys of working on this book has been the opportunity to meet two men who are widely acknowledged to have made very significant contributions to knowledge in the fields of sales and marketing. The first of these is the best-selling business writer, Neil Rackham. As will become clear to any reader of this book, Rackham has become something of a "guru" for me and Minett Media. Part of my work in this book has been to extend some of the ideas he developed for the sales force into the area of B2B marketing. We were able to spend a very convivial – and to me useful – afternoon discussing these issues at his home in Virginia. The second person I want to acknowledge in this category is Prof Evert Gummesson, winner of The American Marketing Association's Award for Outstanding Contributions to Services Marketing (Year 2000). I was able to meet twice with Prof Gummesson in the (to me) familiar surroundings of Stockholm University. I find his views on marketing very sympathetic and he was willing to listen, with great patience, to mine.

A further great debt of gratitude is particularly due to my pre-publication reviewers; Charles Nixon (Chairman of Cambridge Marketing College), Steve Turner

(Senior Lecturer, Stockholm University) and Steve Hinton (Marketing Support Manager, Ericsson, Stockholm). Many thanks for your comments and suggestions – Steve Turner's, in particular, provoked me to significant re-writing. Dr Henrik Uggla, from Brand Strategy Research & Stockholm University's School of Business, very kindly read the theory part of my branding chapter and provided feedback. My thanks to these four does not, of course, detract from my sole responsibility for any errors of fact or reasoning in what follows.

Finally, my greatest and most heart-felt thanks go to my wife, Gunnel, and my son, Michael. Gunnel's support has gone well beyond wifely duty; she is also a partner in Minett Media, so, in addition to very effectively providing the emotional nurturing that every author needs, she's also been an extremely knowledgeable dialogue partner at every stage of the book's development. As a 16-year-old boy, Michael has shown exceptional levels of tolerance and good humor in the face of the stresses and strains of paternal authorship, even sacrificing several practice sessions on his electric guitar in deference to publication deadlines.

Steve Minett, PhD, *June 2001*
MINETT MEDIA,
6 Middlewatch, Swavesey,
Cambridge CB4 5RN, UK
Tel +44 (0)1954 230 250
Fax : +44 (0)1954 232 019
Email: info@minettmedia.co.uk
Website: http://www.minettmedia.co.uk/

chapter one

THE B2B—B2C DIFFERENCE

defining the paradigm territory

basic premise of this book is that the effective requirements for the marketing of B2B products are fundamentally different from those for consumer products. If B2B marketers fail to recognize this basic difference it can seriously reduce

Characteristic	B2B	B2C
Product nature		
Development	Linear	Cyclical
Driver	Technology	Fashion
Customer orientation		
Motivation	Organizational need	Individual wants/desires
Selection	Objective criteria	Subjective preferences
Decision	Left brain	Right brain
Macro-social		
"Two cultures"	Science	Art
Cultural scope	Global Universal	Culture bound
Professional approach		
Analogies	Legal Medical	Politician Entertainer
Focus	Sales & application cases	Consumer characteristics

Figure 1.1 B2B–B2C differences

the effectiveness of their marketing efforts. My objectives in this book are firstly, to clearly identify the differences with B2C and secondly (given these differences), to articulate a professional paradigm for B2B marketers which both recognizes the differences and provides guidance as to how to address them. (See Figure 1.1 for a diagrammatic summary for the arguments that will be presented in Chapters One and Two.)

A gap in theory

These views have arguably been less recognized in theory than in practice: marketing theorists tend to see the subject as a unitary discipline with B2B requiring merely a few minor variations on the basic (B2C) themes. Malcolm McDonald, for example, claims that the "central ideas of marketing are universal and it makes no difference whether we are marketing furnaces, insurance policies or margarine…the conclusion must be that, apart from differences in emphasis, the principles of marketing apply in exactly the same way."[1] James E. Lynch agrees that at "the conceptual level, the central thrust of marketing is relevant to all markets where there are customers, competitors and environmental change… the centrality of the customer is as relevant in industrial or business-to-business markets as it is in consumer goods markets. Equally, the central elements in the marketing process also have universal application."[2] He does, however, recognize certain special characteristics for B2B:

- typically bigger value/bigger unit purchases
- more technically complex products

my objectives in this book

are firstly, to clearly identify the differences with B2C and, secondly (given these differences), to articulate a professional paradigm for B2B marketers which both recognizes the differences and provides guidance as to how to address them

- higher buyer risk

- longer buy times

- more complex decision-making units

- professional purchasers

- closer buyer-seller relationships

- derived demand

- reciprocity.

Adding that, "this list is not comprehensive." A similar list can be found in Thomas L. Power's *Modern Business Marketing.*[3]

While I can agree that satisfying the customer is central to all forms of marketing, the real questions start after this point – "how do *I* satisfy *my* customer?" It's here that the B2B–B2C differences really start. The items on the list above may all be true and relevant, but I'd like to suggest that encouraging B2B practitioners to "bear such lists in mind" while applying the "universal" "...central ideas of marketing" is not the most optimal means of preparing them for their special tasks. B2B practitioners need more than lists of "special characteristics" or "emphases." What they need is a distinct professional identity which differentiates them from B2C practitioners (who have up to now had the predominant role in the marketing profession). They need a clear conceptual map of how their territory differs from that of their consumer-oriented colleagues. They need a paradigm for B2B marketing – ultimately, this is a question of professional effectiveness.

Distinct professional paradigms

Professional paradigms enable practitioners to conceptualize the nature of their subject matter, to understand their practice within this context and to differentiate themselves from other professions, or sub-divisions within a profession. Such paradigms emerge historically with the development of a particular field of human activity; at the beginning of the modern era, science emerged as a distinct professional activity from philosophy. Its traditional branches of physics, biology, and chemistry have now evolved numerous sub-disciplines, such as astro-physics, micro-biology, organic chemistry, etc. The traditional professions of law and medicine now have numerous, specialist sub-divisions and these may often involve quite distinct professional paradigms; for example a surgeon and a psycho-analytically oriented psychiatrist may both be medical doctors but each will approach her task via a completely different conceptual world and will apply their professional knowledge using completely different techniques.

DEFINING THE PARADIGM BOUNDARIES

What I would like to suggest in this book is that marketing, although a very new profession, has reached a point of development at which a distinct professional paradigm for B2B marketers (distinct, that is, from B2C marketers) can now be accepted. The boundaries of the B2B paradigm can be defined by two dimensions of the marketing process; firstly, by the forces which drive companies in their product-market development processes and secondly, by the processes by which customers make their purchase decisions (see Figure 1.2). Looking at this figure, we see that the diametrically opposed boxes "Technology/Formal Organization" and "Fashion/Individual," define the core "paradigm areas," respectively of B2B and B2C. As per conventional wisdom, the focus in the "B2C box" is on the consumer; socio-demographics, life-style profiling, etc. In the "B2B box," I'm suggesting that the focus ought to be on the "case," hence my introduction in this book of the term "case-based marketing," which I suggest is the best-adapted approach for the B2B marketing paradigm. The meaning of "case" will hopefully become clearer during the course of the book, but briefly it refers to the particular application need which a B2B customer has identified and to the *story* of how a solution was eventually found to satisfy this need.

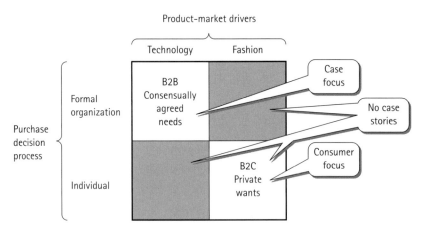

Figure 1.2 Two dimensions of the paradigm

It should also be noted that the figure presents two additional boxes Technology/Individual and Fashion/Formal Organization. Neither of these is really the province of this book. We can, however, briefly observe that the first of these is the more densely populated with transactions; for example home computers, electronics goods, etc. In the context of this book, however, an important point to note about the Technology/Individual box is that *case stories* are not generated within it to anywhere near the extent that they are in the Technology/Formal Organization box. The Fashion/Formal Organization box has a very sparse population; company give-aways being the most obvious example. I should also make a terminological clarification at this point. I'm using the terms technology and fashion as more or less synonymous with utilitarian and self-expressive (which are also used in the marketing literature in these contexts), in the sense of:

- products designed to satisfy consensually agreed needs or to solve practical, objective problems

- products selected by a consumer in order to express their personal characteristics and/or their values.

The "mid-range" B2B purchase

Another piece of "territory clarification" for this book concerns what can be called the "range of B2B purchase" (see Figure 1.3). Clearly, the scale of purchases made by business organizations ranges from the trivial, say a dozen screws or half a dozen pencils, up to major, crucial investments, e.g. constructing a brand new, multi-million-dollar, production plant. Given this context, the focus of this book is on "mid-range purchases," an illustration would be the acquisition of a significant piece of equipment, such as a pump. The idea here is that this is the heartland of B2B marketing: at the trivial end of the range, the products involved tend to be seen as

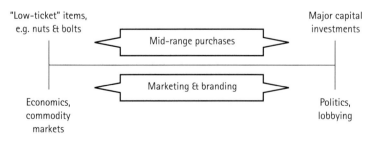

Figure 1.3 B2B purchasing range

commodities and, consequently, the purchasing decision may be predominantly influenced by price. (Though, as we shall see later, the "knowledge-competence" of the customer is also an important prerequisite.) At this end of the range, therefore, the basic principles of classical economics (supply and demand, etc.) apply. At the other extreme, where major capital investments (such as infrastructure for national telecoms systems) are concerned, politics is likely to have a dominant (if not pre-dominant) influence on the decision.

The suggestion is, then, that the scope for effective B2B marketing lies in the middle territory between these two extremes. In this middle territory, risk and uncertainty are high enough to prevent price from being the obvious arbiter, while the consequences of the decision are not significant enough to have major socio-economic impacts on the company and its related communities. This is, in fact, the territory of the "application case" where all parties involved in the transaction engage with each other in solution-oriented dialogues, thereby generating a *case story*. Consequently, this is where *branding* is effective in B2B transactions. As suggested in Figure 1.3, once brand loyalty has developed in this mid-territory, it's possible that it will have "spill-over" effects on transactions at the extremes: an obvious example would be the purchase of basic spare parts. Very simple parts, such as nuts and bolts, can be purchased as commodities, but the stronger the brand-bond, the more likely it is that the customer will turn to the original supplier for all such needs. At the other end the effect may be more erratic: clearly the brand loyalties of employees may well have some influence, but at this level of decision-making they can be over-ridden by macro-political considerations. (For example, in industries such as defence, aerospace, and telecoms, there may be implicit governmental policies regarding the geo-political origin of equipment, e.g. European/American suppliers only.)

TWO TERRITORIAL DIMENSIONS: THE NATURE OF THE PRODUCT AND THE PURCHASING PROCESS

We'll look at the ways in which the two categories of product satisfy their respective customers' needs and wants. I'm going to argue that (in its purest forms) B2B product development is driven by technological progress while for consumer products the driving force is changes in fashion trends, and that, given these different market drivers, their respective prospect and customer groups perceive and behave toward the product in significantly different ways. On the second dimension, I'll consider the contrasting patterns of decision-making employed by B2B and consumer prospects

B2B product development **is driven**
by technological progress while
for consumer products **the driving force** is
changes in **fashion trends**

in their purchasing behavior. The basic theme here is that B2B purchasing takes place within the context of formal organizations, whereas consumer purchasing behavior is either purely individualistic or takes place in extremely small and informal groups such as families and couples.

DIMENSION ONE: TECHNOLOGY- VS FASHION- DRIVEN PRODUCTS – SATISFYING OBJECTIVE NEEDS VS SUBJECTIVE DESIRES

Looking first at the product-market dimension, a spectrum of product-market drivers (see Figure 1.4) is a useful conceptual tool to illustrate the differences. This has technological development at one end and fashion (or "self-expression") at the other. (The concept of the "technology driven" product should not be confused with the idea – well-known within marketing – of a product's development being driven purely by technological development to the exclusion of marketing considerations. What I'm arguing is rather that the developmental input mix for a product can vary from extremely high technological input at one end of the spectrum to extremely high fashion considerations at the other and that the balance of this mix will affect the way in which the product *ought to be* marketed.) The idea of using a spectrum is that these end points represent the ideal typical extremes: products in the real world will always be located somewhere between these extremes.

We can start by looking at typical product locations along this spectrum. Cosmetics, for example, can be located very close to the ideal typical fashion end of the spectrum, given that they are driven almost entirely by unmediated personal preferences: individuals either like a perfume or they don't. It's highly unlikely that anyone, in making this choice, is going to be swayed by technical information about

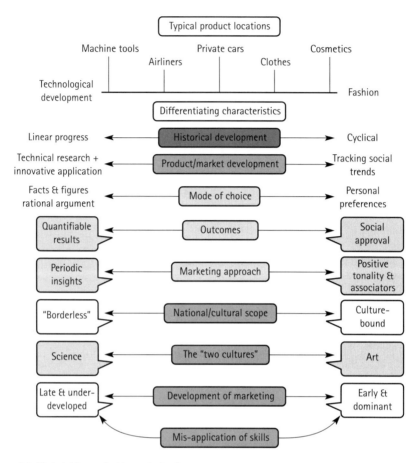

Figure 1.4 Market drivers – fashion vs technology

the product; say by presenting them with the chemical formula of the perfume. (In response to an earlier presentation of this argument, a questioner cited the example of Body Shop. My response to this is that Body Shop's information to customers is much more concerned with *values* – issues such as: natural/traditional ingredients, animal welfare, fair trade, feminism, etc., which would come under the brand element category "value resonance" (see Chapter 4, page 105). My point, I feel, stands – informing a consumer about how a perfume works chemically is not going to change their mind if they don't like the way it smells.) As a long-standing executive in the perfume business once commented, "perfumes are dreams in a bottle." The composition of the fluid is not important. What counts in perfume-purchasing behavior are the highly subjective and idiosyncratic responses which the scent evokes in a prospect. (Of course, these may have been significantly influenced by imagery from advertising before the actual sensory experience takes place, but if this experience is unsatisfactory to the prospect they are unlikely to buy the perfume.)

At the other end of the spectrum, a product group which can be located very close to the ideal-typical, technology-driven end is machine tools. In contrast to perfumes, prospects here are very much interested in technical information about the product, e.g. how the machine has been engineered, what materials were used in its construction, what processes are involved in its functioning, etc. Typically, the prospect here is looking for trade-offs between price and the maximizing of benefits, defined in terms of capacity, efficiency, energy consumption, etc. Technical information about the product is gathered in an effort to evaluate the validity of the vendor's claims. (This should not be taken to imply either that this evaluation is thoroughly and exclusively "rational" nor that it's the only factor in B2B purchasing – see Decision-making at page 63.)

An interesting product example in this context is the mass-produced private car. These days it can be located in the middle of the spectrum, though when it first appeared (in the form of Henry Ford's Model "T") it was much closer to the technology end. The Model "T" was essentially a low-cost machine for getting from A to B. Customers had minimal choice in regard to features: "...any colour you want as long as it's black." Since those days, however, the car has moved progressively towards the fashion end – probably because the differentiation in technological competence between the major manufacturers has been increasingly reduced. Consequently, competition shifts focus onto fashion-driven differentiators, such as body styling, color range, personalized features, etc. At the extreme, we now have overtly fashion-oriented concept cars, which are acquired and used very much like other branded, quasi-fashion accessories, such as watches and mobile phones. (It can be argued that a similar development is taking place in computers, especially portable models.)

To illustrate other positions on the technology-fashion spectrum, we can locate clothing mid-way on the fashion side and planes in a correspondingly middle position on the technology side. The idea here is that in the product's mix of fashion and technology drivers, one type of driver predominates but elements of the other are clearly present. For example, the clothing industry is clearly predominantly driven by fashion, yet its development occasionally manifests examples of technological breakthroughs, such as the zip, Velcro, and more recently, *GoreTex*.

At this point a questioner once raised the example of Benetton, claiming that they demonstrate the reality "that fashion and technology are interlinked" – (apparently) contrary to my simplistically bipolar view. His argument was that Benetton's customers of technology driven products are most likely asking themselves, **"is this product going to work in the way that the vendor claims that it will?"** whereas the fashion-driven product's customer asks, **"is this product consistent with my life-style aspirations and will it communicate them to the people whose opinion is important to me?"**

"technical expertise enables them to change designs within weeks, when Marks & Spencers take up to two years." My response to this is: yes, but do Benetton's *customers* care about Benetton's *production* technology? What they want is the up-to-date fashionableness of Benetton's *products*. Of course, rapid-response, production technology provides Benetton with a marketing advantage – but this has nothing to do with the argument I'm making here – I'm looking at these issues from the *customer's perspective*. My point is that there is a very wide spectrum of *product-related issues* which customers consider when assessing products. What I'm suggesting is that these issues can be conceptually arranged along this spectrum with technological issues (which tend to predominate for buyers in Figure 1.2's "B2B box") at one end and "fashionability" issues (which tend to predominate for buyers in the "B2C box") at the other. A simplistic way of summarizing these two customer approaches is to say that the customers of technology driven products are most likely asking themselves, "is this product going to work in the way that the vendor claims that it will?" whereas the fashion-driven product's customer asks, "is this product consistent with my life-style aspirations and will it communicate them to the people whose opinion is important to me?" See the case opposite for an example of what the difference between the product working and not working can mean to a B2B customer.

Sandvik Rock tools contribute to world's largest, long-wall, coal panels

A long-wall, coal mine in North America has been extracting 6-million-ton panels – the biggest in the world. Initial problems with the blocks holding the bits in the cutter drums were solved when the mine switched to Sandvik's System PR 110. The dimensions of these "panels," i.e. the rectangular sections it extracts from the coal seam in one continuous, back and forth, long-wall operation, are as follows; 8 to 10 feet high, 850 feet long and 15,000 to 20,000 feet long. Each of these panels contains about 6 million tons of coal, the extraction of which requires nine months of work.

Cost-effective

The motivation for cutting these very large panels is very simple, as the mine manager explains: "it costs $2 million to change from one panel to another, for the obvious reasons that we have to cut new access tunnels, move the long-wall shearer, etc... Clearly, the fewer the times we need to do this the more cost-effective our operations will be." Irresistible as this economic logic is, there are, though, problems involved in extracting such large panels: the main constraint on operating panels this large is the wear and tear on the equipment. The mine uses a long-wall shearer equipped with two cutter drums mounted on ranging arms. Each drum is equipped with 63 drill bits. "Before we started cutting these really big panels, we'd been experiencing problems with the blocks, or toolholders, on which these bits are mounted: the impacts transmitted through the bits were causing wear on the blocks such that the bits became loose and or even fell out. As a consequence of this, production had to be stopped and the failed block had to be cut out" (the blocks are welded in place on the cutter drums), "and a new block had to be welded in."

This was a difficult repair job: firstly, the work had to be carried out underground because it is very difficult to remove either the drums from the shearer or the shearer from the mine. Secondly, because each bit has to be very carefully aligned, so that it has the correct "angle of attack." As a result of these difficulties it was taking 8 to 10 hours to replace each block that failed. In addition, after cutting about 2 million tons or so a whole drum would have to be replaced. This also took between 8 to 10 hours and cost approximately $60,000. The mine manager adds that, "Apart from the cost of the work and the parts, there's also, of course, the loss of production that this downtime causes. For us this amounts to $500 per minute, or $80,000 per shift."

Switch To Sandvik bits

The solution to these problems proved to be a switch to Sandvik's RP 110 drill bits. The critical factors which enable the System RP 110 to overcome these block failure problems are described by Sandvik's sales representative to the mine as follows: "firstly, there's a shoulder or 'skirt' around the bit which covers and rests on most of the block surface when the bit is inserted into it. This shoulder has the effect of spreading the impacts over the whole block, thus reducing the point stress. Secondly, the RP 110 has somewhat larger shaft dimensions than a conventional cutting tool of this type; its shaft is 55 mm by 35 mm compared with the more conventional size of 50 mm by 30 mm. The larger sized shaft provides additional strength and wear resistance. Also all sharp corners have been eliminated from the shaft design, which again means that loads are dispersed over a larger area. Thirdly, it's got a robust locking device which gives full contact across the width of the tool and toolholder, providing a very secure retaining method."

Cost savings

"We've completed two 6-million ton panels using Sandvik's RP 110 system," says the mine manager, "and we've experienced no block failure problems. In terms of cost savings for the replacement of bits alone, this amounts to about $100,000. He adds that, "without these bits the productivity of our large panels would have been greatly reduced." Calculations carried out on the mine's operating costs also indicate the following: in terms of dollars per ton of coal mined, the RP 110 costs $0.025 per ton whereas the non-Sandvik bits which the mine used previously cost $0.035 per ton.

This detailed presentation of a product's features, in this case, may fly in the face of conventional marketing wisdom – "present *benefits* not features!" – my argument, however, is that it's highly desirable in B2B marketing. B2B customers are rarely impressed by a bald statement of benefit: "these drill bits will success-fully withstand extremely heavy usage." They also want a technical explanation as to why this should be the case.

An example of a product located between the technology end and the mid-point is the airliner: the product development of planes is (for very obvious reasons) pre-dominantly driven by technological developments. But, given the intensification of competition between airlines, many of their features (especially of course in the passenger cabins) are now driven by fashion trends in terms of color schemes, light-ing, entertainment systems, etc. Airlines select these things on the basis of what they believe will be the preferences of *their* customers.

Linear progress vs cyclical trends

Having described this basic dichotomy between technology and fashion as market drivers, we can now look at some of the more nuanced characteristics which differ-entiate them. There's a general consensus that the history of technology is characterized by linear progress. (Underlying this is the idea that knowledge in the natural sciences accumulates according to criteria of utility, given that, in modern societies, technology develops via the practical application of scientific knowledge.) This means that, we acquire more and more accurate knowledge about natural processes which enables us to make quantitative steps forward in our technological prowess – we can travel faster, compute larger quantities of data, move greater vol-umes of earth and rock, etc.

We can contrast this concept of gradual, linear, cumulative progress in technol-ogy with the history of fashion. Developments here do not move in a linear direction; fashion trends come, go, and (may possibly) return. Flared trousers and the platform shoe provide recent examples of the cyclical development of fashion. Given this, product and market development for individual manufacturers of fash-ion products need to be driven by their close tracking of social trends (if they're going to be successful). In contrast, the development of technology-driven prod-ucts is ultimately linked to discoveries in scientific research, i.e. to a totally different sphere of human activity. The example overleaf is based on developments in micro-processing combined with the principles of electro-mechanics.

☀ Variable speed pumps can save 70% of energy consumed

Major energy savings can be made by simply enabling pumps to run at variable speeds instead of a single fixed speed – up to 70%. About 80% of pumps are still constant speed units so the scope for energy saving worldwide is huge. ITT Vogel has introduced a "smart" speed control system, based on pump-mounted micro-processors.

The car analogy

Constant-speed pumps operate very much as if a car driver had one foot constantly flat down on the accelerator and was using the brakes to control the car's speed. In contrast, ITT's Hydrovar system is like a car with an automatic gearbox – including cruise control. With a constant-speed pump there are basically three flow control methods. Firstly, the flow can be reduced mechanically by throttling the discharge or returning excess flow to the suction side of the pump. Secondly, a by-pass system can reduce the flow to the pump; apart from wasting energy, this system can induce cavitation in the impeller causing additional wear. Thirdly, hydraulic accumulators can be used to absorb excess flow and store it under pressure. When the pump output drops below demand, the accumulator can be used to bring the flow up to the desired level, but accumulators are expensive, take up space, have limited capacity and seldom produce a smooth and constant flow.

Frequency conversion

The speed of a simple induction motor depends on the frequency of the AC power supplying it. In most of Europe mains supply is at 50 Hz (cycles per second) and in the United States 60 Hz, so motors connected directly to the mains turn at multiples of these figures depending on how the motor is wound. To alter the frequency of the motor supply and thus regulate pump speed, the Hydrovar system rectifies the mains supply to DC and then inverts it under command from the controller to provide the frequency required to match pump demand. Input to the frequency controller comes from pressure and flow sensors; these inputs are integrated with the operator's program to provide a fully flexible operating regime.

The spread of the variable-speed pump throughout industry might loosely be described as a "technological fashion trend." However, what distinguishes this development from a *real* fashion trend is that (given the economic advantages of these products) the chances of the fixed-speed pump making a "come-back" are virtually zero.

So, there is a clear difference between technology-driven products, which arise out of technical research and its innovative application, and fashion-driven products, whose development depends on tracking social trends, i.e. being sensitive to the way life-styles are developing, the way people's values are changing, etc. But what about customers? How do their choice criteria differ between technology and fashion products? We can look both at pre-purchase evaluation and at post-purchase outcomes.

Pre-purchase evaluation

Our argument is that fashion products are mainly concerned with social communication, with a view to eliciting social approval (not necessarily from "society at large"; more likely from peer groups whose good opinion is important to the consumer in question). In making a product selection for these purposes, a consumer has to rely on personal preference – as only they really know what sort of self-image they wish to project – and as these processes may very often be taking place at a sub-conscious level, these preferences will frequently be experienced as "gut level" reactions.

Things are, however, different at the technology end of the spectrum. This is not to argue that product selection on the technology side is always carried out by a rigorously, and objectively, rational process. Our argument is rather that it's conducted within an ideology of rational choice, involving public rational discourse – which is not quite the same thing. The idea here is that when buying technology-driven products, especially in a B2B context, people want to have facts and figures about the product; they want to engage in rational argument about how it works and what sort of performance it can deliver. They are also likely to want to make at least some effort to compare competitive product offerings in terms of these objective criteria.

Post-purchase outcomes

We can now consider the differences in outcome from purchasing decisions. With a fashion product, the best case outcome is that the purchaser does, in fact, enjoy the social approval whose pursuit drove them to purchase it in the first place. If this is not the case – if when they first expose the product to "social scrutiny" they experience an uncomfortable feeling of disapproval from those whose opinion is important to them – then they may deem the purchase a mistake. This is not due to any technical failure in the product. (Poor quality in production leading to mechanical failures in the product is a separate issue.) What's happened is that the manufacturer or the consumer (or possibly both) have got the social signaling "wrong" for the particular group they were targeting. It's interesting to note that despite regarding the purchase as a failure, a consumer is unlikely to complain about this type of product failure to the manufacturer.

Again, the contrast with technology products is clear: technology purchasers may have established precise and explicit performance criteria for the product before they purchased it. Success would, obviously, consist of the product consistently meeting or exceeding these criteria, whereas customer dissatisfaction would arise from its failure to do so. These criteria will very often be quantifiable – a percentage reduction in energy consumption, a percentage increase in efficiency or productivity, etc. The *Zinc Mine* case below provides a real-life example. Customers in this context are not going to feel coy about complaining to the manufacturer about such objectively definable failures.

Zinc mine upgrades production and quality with high-capacity flotation cells

The challenge for this zinc ore processing plant was to expand its extraction capabilities, due to a higher metallic content in the mined ore. But the company wanted to do this without having to rebuild or dramatically extend its plant. The answer was to install 22 higher-capacity Svedala flotation units.

The current plant was designed for ore with a zinc content of 8% and a lead content of 1.5%. Now however, due partly to better mining techniques but also to the discovery of better quality ore, the zinc content is 10–11% and the lead content is 4–4.5%. In order to extract this higher metallic content, higher retention times are required in the flotation process, i.e. more cells of the same capacity and process time, or a similar number of larger cells in which the ore would be retained longer.

The mine manager explains: "The alternatives were to build more lines with cells the size of the existing ones, or to buy equipment with larger capacity cells. We went for the latter option. Around the same time Svedala was field testing its RCS flotation unit." Svedala's senior applications engineer, says: "We approached the mine with a request to install it for test purposes. The mine, consequently, had two equivalent units operating side-by-side, so it was easy to compare their performance." The mine manager says, "With the Svedala unit we were getting better recovery of fine particles, and fine particles are characteristic of the ore process at the mine. Another advantage with big flotation cells in Svedala's units is that they have fewer working parts, which impacts favorably on service and maintenance time and costs, and on energy consumption." The two factors are linked. Svedala's engineer explains: "The better recovery of fine particles is due to the design of the impeller diffuser mechanism in each of the Svedala RCS flotation cells."

The mine eventually bought 22 of Svedala's RCS flotation cell units and the results are good. "We used to have a problem with excessive silica in the zinc concentrate," the manager explains, "When we delivered the concentrate we had to pay penalties for having a silica content over a certain level, but since using the Svedala equipment we have been able to reduce the silica content by approximately 1%. We have also improved the recovery rates from the ore, and the grade of the concentrate, by about 1% each. The old recovery rate was 94% and it is now risen to 95, and the old grade was 55% and is now risen to 56."

Discussions with an English marketing colleague raised objections to the discussion above: "What about," he suggested, "the person who wants to 'make an impression' at work or at the local yacht club? They might well go to their tailor or regular clothes shop and specifically ask for advice on this topic. If they take this advice and then experience the clothes in question as failing to impress in the desired way, they might well go back and complain about it." My response to this is twofold: firstly, this situation really takes us out of Figure 1.2's Individual/Fashion box and into its Individual/Technology box, i.e. it turns fashion choice into a technological problem – which I can agree, in many cases (especially in conservative workplaces) it is. Secondly,

a good way to make a splash at a Washington cocktail party would be to turn up wearing a purple wet suit.

my feeling is that, as a critique of the description above, this is a rather culture-bound perspective (both in the English and the traditional senses): fashion in post-modern societies is becoming much more concerned with expressing idiosyncratic personal identities (often associated with one or more of the very many sub-cultures which flourish in our pluralistic societies) than with social conformity. This post-modernist spirit is epitomized by the psychologist, Wayne Dyer, who suggests that a good way to make a splash at a Washington cocktail party would be to turn up wearing a purple wet suit.

Difference in marketing approach

Having considered these differences between technology and fashion driven products, we can now look at what influence these "product-market" differences should have on our respective approaches to marketing them. Given the nature of technology products, as described above, it can be concluded that the presentation of objective information, often of some complexity, is required in their marketing. This type of marketing could be defined as a pedagogic activity – educating potential customers as to the quantifiable benefits to be achieved from a particular product – aimed at inducing insights about how the product works. With fashion products, however, their marketing is much more concerned with the cultivation of positive associations for the product in the minds of consumers. As an example of the B2B pedagogic approach, see the product presentation opposite.

☼ "Artificial respiration" for lakes

The quality of water, especially in terms of oxygen content, is today often being badly affected by the growing amount of organic material that accumulates in lakes and other bodies of water. Technological systems, involving mixers and pumps, to mechanically circulate the water, may, however, be able to provide a solution. In their natural state lakes, and other large bodies of water, are self-maintaining ecological systems. Their oxygen content is naturally regulated at an optimal level and bacteria, on the bed of the lake, efficiently dispose of whatever biological debris may accumulate in them. The bacteria use up oxygen in the process of digesting the organic material but this is replaced by the lake's natural "breathing" mechanism: oxygen from the atmosphere is absorbed at the water surface, which is normally oxygen-saturated. If the oxygen content at the surface is lowered, oxygen transfer increases, resulting in a total net input of oxygen into the "epilimnion," the warmer water at the top of the lake. This then transfers oxygen to the "hypolimnion," the cooler water at the bottom of the lake. The water in lakes is divided into these two bodies by a distinct drop in temperature which occurs suddenly at a particular depth in the water. This line in the water is known as the "thermocline."

Enter pollution

In industrialized societies, however, this self-regulating balance has been disturbed. The main culprits are the nutrient compounds, such as potassium, nitrates, and phosphates, which modern societies generate in abundance. They find their way into lakes from two principal sources; firstly from the fertilizers used in modern agriculture and, secondly, in the discharge from sewage treatment plants. The nutrients give rise to increased bio-activity, uncontrolled growth of algae and bottom vegetation, which eventually die and settle at the bottom. This enormous increase in the quantity of organic material accumulating in lakes can threaten their ecological balance: the bacteria, at the bottom of the lake, which digest these compounds consume oxygen during the process. As the quantity of material increases so do the populations of these bacteria and, consequently the amount of oxygen which they extract from the water. A point is reached at which they totally deplete the oxygen content of the hypolimnion. Since the two layers (the epilimnion and the hypolimnion) are stratified, the exchange of oxygen-rich surface water into the hypolimnion is hindered. When the oxygen in the hypolimnion has been exhausted, this lower body of water can no longer sustain any higher life-forms and the lake bottom becomes biologically "dead." Even before this terminal point is reach, however, such unhealthy developments produce disturbing and ecologically damaging symptoms: the anaerobic bacterial activity produces an excess of methane gas which rises to the surfaces. This can poison fish, even at surface levels, and gives rise to an unpleasant smell.

Technological solution

The long-term solution to this problem is to reduce the quantity of nutrients finding their way into water bodies to a level that does not disturb their ecological balance. In the short-term there are technical solutions available; methods which use improved circulation and exchange of water to increase the natural digestive capacities of nutrient-overloaded water bodies. These techniques involve transporting large quantities of water across the thermocline, into the epilimnion. The water in the epilimnion circulates to the surface and, consequently, is always oxygen-rich. The transfer of additional water into the epilimnion has two effects: firstly, it lowers the level of the thermocline, which means that oxygen-containing water reaches deeper into the lake. Secondly, it increases the water exchange rate between the oxygen-rich epilimnion and the oxygen-depleted hypolimnion. This can be described as "artificial respiration" for lakes. The water transfer required is achieved with submersible mixers and/or pumps. They enable large quantities of water to be exchanged in the bottom zone at relatively low cost, in terms of both capital investment and energy consumption.

(For a practical application of this technique, see the *Japanese Golf Club Case* on page 184.)

This difference between technology and fashion products raises the question of the national or cultural scope of the two varieties of marketing effort: the prospects for fashion products are likely to be asking themselves (explicitly or implicitly), "is this

technology driven products have the potential to be marketed in a truly borderless way

product fashionable?" It's fairly obvious that the answer to this question is likely to vary from country to country and from culture to culture – even between regions in the same country. There are, of course, counter-trends in the contemporary world: young people in particular, under the influence of such developments as the globalization of popular music and the spread of satellite and cable TV, seem to be evolving a planetary consensus about what is currently fashionable. However, this "global fashion village" is very much confined to the westernized, post-industrial world. As an obvious illustration, it could be commented that the use of explicit sexual imagery may well promote a product in the West but in, for example, a Muslim fundamentalist society like Iran it would very definitely be counter-productive.

Borderless technology

Technology driven products have the potential to be marketed in a truly borderless way. There are two reasons for this: firstly (as we have seen), there's a lot of scope for the use of rational arguments and quantifiable information in their marketing, which appeals beyond the confines of particular ethnic, national, or religious cultures. Secondly, over the last two hundred or so years, the modern business organization has evolved, an "ideology of rationality." This means that within organizations there is a preference for the use of "rational," "objective" and (ideally) quantifiable information in their decision-making processes. (To repeat, this does not, of course, mean that all organizational decisions are totally rational – hence the use of the word "ideology.") This ideology of rationality is spreading globally under the influence of two forces: at the macro-level, the spread of free-market capitalism through the liberalization of previously communist or reactionary regimes. This has the effect of weeding out, via a competitive market, organizations which consistently ignore rational arguments. Secondly, at the micro-level, the globalization of modern business organization: through ownership or intensified trading across borders, business actors the world over, irrespective of their cultural and geographic backgrounds, are adapting to the modern organization's central ideology of rationality (at least while making B2B decisions at work).

Let's now look at the second major dimension of the B2B paradigm – purchasing behavior. We've already considered, to some extent, how consumer and B2B transactions differ from each other. Here I'd like to introduce a model, based on the bicameral brain, to illustrate how these differences actually manifest themselves in the decision-making process. Secondly, I want to emphasize the point that B2B decisions always – implicitly or explicitly – involve groups of people whereas consumers make their purchases as individuals. We can then consider what consequences this has for the various actors.

The bicameral brain

The, now well-established, bicameral model of the brain postulates that the obvious anatomical division of the brain into a right and left half also reflects a functional division in its operation: the left side is genetically designed to deal with what could be called the "hard" aspects of mental life: logic, calculation, and analysis, whereas the right side handles the "soft" side: intuition, images, pattern recognition, etc. Given our discussion of technology/fashion above, the case I want to make here is (simply stated) that the left side of the brain handles the purchasing of technology products and the right side, fashion products. (We'll see later that B2B purchasing,

B2B decisions always –
implicitly or explicitly –
involve groups of people whereas consumers make
their purchases as individuals

in particular, is more complex than this – but this is the basic argument.) I can also anticipate here a proposition about marketing communications (which I'll present fully later), that, as a result of this basic division of brain function, the right side tends to respond to the advertising channel (including direct mail, etc.), while the left side is employed to evaluate messages in the editorial channel.

Figure 1.5 considers a simple consumer purchase, such as a cosmetic (i.e. a product very close to the ideal-typical fashion end of our spectrum). A classic pattern for the first purchase of such an extreme-consumer product could proceed as follows: an individual might first encounter this product in an advertisement, perhaps even at the point of sale. The advertisement's images and copy may trigger attractive associations in the right side of the individual's brain, such that they may feel an immediate impulse to buy the product, even though they had never felt any previous need for it. (Here it's instructive to note that the emphasis in advertising of this type is overwhelmingly on images. Such advertisements tend to be very short on words and the words that are there are intended to elicit feelings and associations rather than to convey information.) As a result of this right-side response, the individual may immediately purchase the product. If the right side's positive response has been very strong, the left side of the brain may not be engaged in the process at all. Alternatively, if the response was weaker, or if the consumer is cautious, the left side's role may simply be to consider whether the price of the product is consistent with the individual's disposable income.

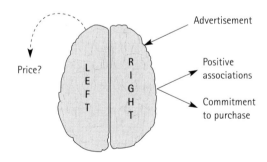

Figure 1.5 Simple consumer purchase

The B2B purchasing process

We can contrast this with a typical B2B purchasing process. In terms of the bicameral brain, a summary of this process could be imagined as follows: having recognized a need for a particular type of product, the customer will then initiate a search for information as to what alternatives are available. Next, information on the nature of the offer for each alternative will be gathered and evaluated. (The extent and thoroughness of the information search and analysis will vary between both individual customers and the significance of the proposed purchase.) The information search and analysis activities are conducted on the left side of the brain, but (significantly) the argument here is that the actual decision to purchase and the commitment to remain loyal to a particular brand (which can be described as a leap of faith) are right-side phenomena – even in the case of B2B goods. Once this commitment has been made in B2B purchasing, it then has to be justified to the purchasing group – which requires a return to left-side information analysis (see Figure 1.6).

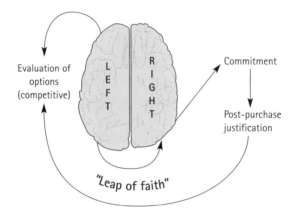

Figure 1.6 B2B purchasing: a leap of faith plus justification

Our analysis requires a much more detailed account of B2B purchasing: what follows has been adapted from the work of Neil Rackham[4] (complemented by personal discussion with him). Unlike most other "sales gurus," Rackham emphasizes from the start that what is important is not to develop a strategy of selling, but to deeply and fully understand the process by which B2B purchasers make their decisions. In truth, therefore, his model could more accurately be called a "B2B Purchasing Model." The model clearly recognizes the "organizational dimension" of B2B buying: he talks about the "purchasing channel" which consists of the following actors – gate keepers, influencers, decision-makers and sponsors, and has three "focuses" (which are individuals or sub-groups within the organization which have an influence on purchasing decisions). These are:

- the focus of receptivity

- the focus of dissatisfaction and

- the focus of power.

The dynamic part of the model is Rackham's version of the customer decision process. He divides this into four phases:

- the recognition of need

- evaluation of options

- resolution of concerns and

- implementation.

Need recognition

The recognition of need arises when customers feel an acute dissatisfaction with the methods, systems, products, and/or suppliers on which they have been previously relying. (See the case study below on a manufacturer of cutting tools.) Here, immediately, the group nature of B2B purchasing becomes significant: in the case of a major equipment purchase (or the initiation of a pattern of serial purchases), it's highly unlikely that a single individual within an organization would decide what was needed without any consultation, discussion, and agreement with others in the organization. The fact that such discussions take place during the B2B recognition of need phase, makes this a left-side brain function. Rackham identifies selling strategies for each of his phases and in the recognition of needs phase the strategy is to uncover and intensify the dissatisfaction felt by the prospective customer. Ideally, this should be selectively channelled towards the product benefits that the seller's company has to offer.

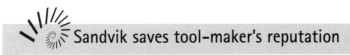

Sandvik saves tool-maker's reputation

An American manufacturer of cutting tools saved its reputation by changing its supplier of blanks. The unreliability of its previous, bought-in blanks resulted in a loss of production – and some customers.

Increasing dissatisfaction

The company became increasingly dissatisfied with its supplier of blanks. The company's president recalled the difficulties. "We were having problems with consistency in a number of batches," he says. "They could be divided into three categories: firstly, the blanks which were center-less ground by a subcontractor, were coming in over-sized. Originally we didn't inspect for this and we ended up making complete tools which were also oversized. When we discovered this was happening, we had to inspect every piece. Secondly, they often couldn't supply us with the exact sizes we wanted from stock so they were having pieces cut to size. This activity was also subcontracted and we discovered that these sizes too were not reliable. Thirdly, and perhaps most seriously, we were experiencing carbide failure in the tools that we supplied to our customers. We were getting returns of broken tools, sending them for laboratory testing and discovering that it was the material which had caused these problems. We lost customers through these failures."

Testing alternative suppliers

The president describes how his company undertook a rigorous and systematic testing process to solve their component supply problems. "First we pre-qualified a number of potential suppliers," he explained. "One issue was price; we wanted to pay the midrange price but obviously we wanted the best specifications available at that price. This process produced a shortlist of four potential suppliers. Then we set up in-house testing using our CNC machines. It was important to use computer control of the machines so that we could get an accurate re-run of the production processes. This meant that the only variable when comparing the performance of the components from the four suppliers was the material itself. We then made three to six boring bars to the same specifications using materials from each of the four suppliers." Other parameters like coolant flow and pressure were also kept the same, ensuring a level playing field for each of the four suppliers. All the tools were then tested on a lathe making a standard number of parts, after which each was examined microscopically.

Better performance

These tests showed that the Sandvik material performed between 10 and 20% better than the previous supplier and about 20 to 30% better than the two other potential suppliers. Another factor which led to the selection of Sandvik was the company's policy of supplying "premium blanks," i.e. the pieces arrived with a high polish finish and already chamfered. The president comments: "When the other suppliers were informed about this they also offered to supply ready cut chamfers – but at a higher price. The Sandvik pieces also proved to be very consistent in size. In fact we've more or less eliminated inspection of these pieces as they come in."

Having established that the need for a new equipment purchase is valid, those responsible within the organization will become receptive to relevant marketing messages. These various messages, from competing suppliers, will reach them, for example, in the form of advertisements in relevant trade journals or via direct mail addressed to them. (Messages which they would normally, i.e. where no need had been recognized, ignore. See Figure 1.7.) In line with our "division of brain labor" above, the use of the advertising channel for these messages moves the process over to the right side.

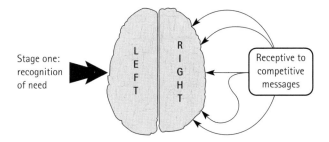

Figure 1.7   B2B purchasing: need and receptiveness

The evaluation of options

Having accumulated information about the relevant competitive offerings, the B2B buyer moves on to stage two, the "evaluation of options." The objective here is to

which of these options is most likely to be capable of fulfilling the need

identify which of these options is most likely to be capable of fulfilling the need which has been established. Rackham suggests that a major step in this stage consists of formulating and rank-ordering the "decision criteria" necessary to make this selection. These decision criteria should embody exactly what the organization wants this (for example) piece of equipment to be able to do and what features it will need to have in order to be able to do this. When this list of criteria has been established, they then need to be arranged in order of importance according to the organization's purposes. Examples of such criteria could be: capacity per hour, speed of operation, speed of set-up, energy consumption, weight, corrosion resistance, temperature range of operation, etc. (See the customer's criteria in the Belgium quarry case study below.)

Modular wear linings – meeting an aggregate supplier's requirements

The Swedish-based mining and construction equipment group Svedala has introduced a modular wear lining system based on manageably sized squares of rubber, polyurethane, and ceramics.

Wear, in industrial applications, is caused by a number of different mechanisms: in chutes, feeders, hoppers, or other transfer components, the form of wear differs at entry and exit. At entry, impact wear predominates while at exit sliding wear is at its greatest. A "tailor-made," uniform lining therefore is unable to give the best performance in all areas.

Svedala, however, has developed a flexible solution via modularity; a system of square modules of different materials each best able to resist a particular type of wear. Thus, in a chute application, rubber modules are fitted at entry to absorb impact and at discharge, ceramic modules are fitted where sliding wear is at a peak. Modularity also has an overwhelming advantage in the initial fitting of the modules and in replacement of those that are worn. Fitting a one-piece molded liner can be a difficult, dangerous, time-consuming, and expensive job if the transfer component is located in an awkward situation. The wear modules, however, can be fitted by one man using only a spanner and a knife. Modularity also permits a trial approach to lining: materials can be installed in various combinations, which can then be reconfigured according to performance. It is likely that only a few modules will need to be changed and this can be done with very little plant downtime.

An aggregate quarry in Belgium

The company produces about 2 million tonnes of aggregate per year. When the quarry's processing plant was upgraded, new hoppers were installed. Trellsquare linings were fitted in these. The material goes through primary and secondary crushing before arriving at the hoppers. They have a through-put of 100 tonnes per hour each. The plant manager recalls that the original hoppers were lined with steel plates only about 10 mm thick which were worn through, often within a week. These were repaired by welding steel plates directly over the holes. Another problem was the build up of materials on the sides of the hoppers, which would often have to be manually cleaned every two days.

"When we looked at constructing the two new hoppers our goals were to get a very long-life lining material and to try to avoid the build up of the material on the sides of the hopper," he says. "We also wanted to use light materials so that we would not need to have a very heavy and expensive structure for the hoppers. We looked at three different possibilities; rubber 20 to 25 mm thick, 'Nihard' steel and polyurethane. In the end we decided on rubber Trellsquares." Calculations showed that the heavy section steel would have required the hopper's structure to be strengthened. It would also have been difficult to install and would have had a life-time of perhaps only between a month and a year. The polyurethane as a total lining solution would have been too expensive.

Prospects' decision criteria – the key to sales

In the evaluation of options phase the objective of selling strategy is to understand and then try to influence the decision criteria which the prospective customer will use to make a choice between alternative options. Rackham comments that a very common error here is failure to fully understand the decision criteria. (This results, as we shall see, in a failure to differentiate the seller's products.) Given the goal of influencing and/or changing decision criteria, Rackham suggests the following procedure: first uncover them. Use very thorough and structured questioning of the prospect in order to establish what decision criteria she is evolving. Secondly, try to influence these criteria and, thirdly, try to maximize the perceived fit between the prospect's decision criteria and the benefits which your company has to offer.

Criteria last for a life time

Rackham emphasizes a very important quality which decision criteria possess – they live on after a particular sale. When purchasers have put in the effort necessary to develop decision criteria for a particular need situation, these are likely to become deeply embedded in their minds: they will, henceforth, tend to use them every time a similar need situation arises in order to make decisions about future purchases, and the influence of these "tried and tested" decision criteria can potentially extend over the entire working life-time of a purchaser. (The obvious marketing benefits of being able to influence decision criteria in a way that favors your products and your company, will be explored in Chapters Two, Seven, and Eight.)

Clearly, one of the most important tasks of a salesperson is to influence the decision criteria of their prospects. Rackham recommends three basic strategies for achieving this; firstly, reinforcing criteria that you can meet. Secondly, building up incidental criteria, i.e. criteria that the buyer either just hasn't thought of at all or, alternatively, has thought about but discarded – maybe prematurely. Thirdly, to reduce the importance of crucial decision criteria which you can't meet. Here Rackham suggests four tactics:

- overtaking
- redefining
- trading off or
- creating alternative solutions.

(We'll look at exactly what these mean – and at their implications for marketing in Chapter Seven.)

Identifying differentiators

During the second stage, the "evaluation of options," the prospective customer will attempt to identify "differentiators" between the various options available. "Differentiators," according to Rackham, must fulfil two requirements; firstly, they must truly differentiate between products, i.e. they have to be based on product features which differ clearly and decisively between the options. For example, the top speed of one machine might be double that of the next fastest, or the motor capacity of the most powerful machine might be double the average power of the others. Secondly, differentiators must be based on the customer's need, i.e. the alternatives should differ from each other in ways which are both relevant to, and important for, the prospective customer. Having established the differentiators of the available options, the prospective customer will then assess their relative importance for their particular application need.

Matching differentiators with decision criteria

The obvious way to do this is to attempt to match the differentiators against the prospect's pre-established decision criteria: for example, if the buyer has previously decided that speed is the most important feature of the new machine that he/she is looking for, while motor capacity is secondary and (given the acute need) price comes third as a consideration, they will probably buy the fastest machine, with an average motor capacity, assuming that they can get it at a price which seems reasonable to them. This option would thus be the best fit between the differentiators and the customer's decision criteria. Rackham points out that in many cases (especially those which involve major capital expenditure for the organization), these processes are explicitly formalized through the formation of a purchasing committee, who then go through these procedures. But even in the absence of this formalization, he argues that all "major account" (i.e. in our terms B2B) buyers will go through these processes in some form or another and at some level of consciousness. See the case study overleaf for an example of this "matching" process, from a sewing machine manufacturer searching for an environmentally friendly component cleaner.

Cleaning precision parts – from chemical solvents to supercritical carbon dioxide

A world leader in sewing machine manufacture faced a problem: the government banned the chemical solvent it used to clean its sintered parts. The solution proved to be supercritical carbon dioxide, which is both a very efficient cleaner and also completely "green." This new method has great potential wherever sintered, or other precision parts are used – especially in the automotive and semi-conductor industries.

This manufacturer produced its own sintered parts, to ensure quality and a regular supply. The process of sintering is based on powder metallurgy. A metallic powder is pressed together in a punch with a die tool. The shaped parts are then sintered for three hours at temperatures of 1120°C. To produce more exact tolerances and shapes of the required components, they are dipped in "sizing" oil before a second pressing, or sizing. A final cleaning phase is needed to remove the sizing oil and any dirt accumulated during the process, which otherwise would create detrimental effects in the final sewing machine.

The problem was this very thorough cleaning, which required the use of trichlorethylene – now banned by legislation. This cleaned the components adequately, but, was not very efficient, and not at all environmentally friendly: the process took four hours at a temperature of 140°C. Only 30 minutes of this was the actual cleaning process, the rest of the time was needed to get rid of the chloroethylene gas. The process produced 400 litres of liquid waste per year and this contained chlorine, which made it very difficult and expensive to dispose of.

The search for green cleaning

The head of mechanical engineering R&D at the plant, explained the various alternatives they looked at in their search for a better – and more environmentally friendly – way to resolve the problem. "First, we looked at using ultrasound combined with cyclohexane, which is a liquid. But the cleaning was not very efficient, and the gas is highly flammable and risky, bearing in mind that the cleaning takes place immediately next to the oven. Then we looked at petroleum ether – but this is very similar to ordinary vehicle fuel and also too risky to use so close to the oven. Also the emissions could not be 100% contained, and so it would have been difficult to get government approval to use it. Next, we looked at water cleaning solutions, but these were not very practical because of the possibility of corrosion and they did not do the job very well."

Then the plant started to consider the use of supercritical carbon dioxide: they made contact with Chematur Engineering AB in Sweden and tested their supercritical carbon dioxide cleaning process which incorporates a unique rotating basket to enhance cleaning efficiency. These results were very good. The sewing machine company was impressed and bought one of Chematur's Rotowasher units (a component cleaning machine which uses supercritical carbon dioxide).

The Rotowasher process

The cleaning process in the Rotowasher is based on dissolving organic contaminants, including oils, in supercritical carbon dioxide at high temperature and pressure. The CO_2 is initially pre-cooled, then compressed and heated to the desired level before being fed to the treatment chamber. A rotating cleaning basket maximizes the cleaning effect by enhancing mass transfer. This unique rotating basket arrangement utilizes centrifugal force to enhance cleaning efficiency.

After dissolving the organic impurities the CO_2 passes through a pressure release valve which is designed to allow a constant mass flow. The pressure of the loaded CO_2 is reduced, and any liquid CO_2 is gasified in the evaporator. The oil contaminants are collected in the bottom separator from where they are removed, and activated carbon filters are used to eliminate any remnant of contaminant from the circulating system. The gaseous CO_2 is then liquefied in a condenser and returns to the storage tank ready to be re-used. The only consumables are carbon dioxide – 2–3 kilo per cleaning operation – and energy. The carbon dioxide can be re-used in the next cleaning operation, and any steel particles from the cleaning process are extracted by a ring shaped magnet. The cleaning process takes an hour for each batch.

"Hard" and "soft" differentiators

When considering competitive differentiators, Rackham comments that these can be divided into two categories: "hard" and "soft." Hard differentiators are the obvious things about a product which can often be quantified – weight, speed, capacity, etc. For purposes of purchasing, the hardest and most obvious of hard differentiators is the price. Soft differentiators are the less obvious, though possibly highly significant benefits that the product's features may be able to offer. There's clearly some kind of relationship between hard/soft differentiators and the more traditional features/benefits dichotomy, which perhaps can be summarized as follows: hard differentiators are the most obvious benefits which a product's features can provide – a machine tool which operates at a higher speed will obviously produce more units per hour, a pump which consumes less power than an alternative pump of the same capacity will obviously be less expensive to operate, etc. In the case below, a Spanish paper plant manager immediately saw two hard differentiators in the CellecoScreen – a 50% reduction in both capital and running costs.

☼ A successful application in Spain for GLV Celleco's "universal" pulp screen

The CellecoScreen uses interchangeable combinations of screen basket and rotor for different applications. It has a patented "angled" screen design, which provides exceptional removal performance. In addition, space-saving service access and a new approach to replaceable parts make it easy and economical to operate. It represents a new generation of market-driven, screen technology. Its design features were developed from extensive market research and customer feedback.

A Spanish paper plant has installed two CellecoScreens. Their number two machine originally only produced sack paper but it has been recently rebuilt to enable it to also produce kraft MG. The CellecoScreens at the plant were both purchased in connection with this rebuilding process. The plant's Production Manager explains: "We were looking for equipment to treat two inlet flows for the reconstructed number two machine. One was required to treat recovered wet strength waste. Our plant produces between 50 and 100 tons of this per month. Previously, this was more or less a waste product, which we had to dispose of in various ways. Now we use it as a feed-stock for the rebuilt number two machine. We mix it with the white waste produced by the machine. Another feed stock for the rebuilt machine is OCC (recycled cardboard containers). These are trucked into the plant and pulped and we needed equipment to carry out fine screening of brown waste arising from this."

One unit Instead of 3 or 4

The production manager's original plan was to construct a treatment line consisting of: high-consistency cleaners, de-flakers and multi-stage, probably two-stage, screening. The multi-stage screening would have required considerable dilution of the flow. Having been introduced to the CellecoScreen, however, he discovered that the functions of this entire line could be carried out by this single piece of equipment. "The capital cost saving here was about 50% and the operation would, of course, be very much simplified but the results would be the same or better." He also comments that energy consumption was significantly reduced by opting for the CellecoScreen: "the treatment line would have consisted of three or four machines plus perhaps three pumps, whereas the CellecoScreen is a single unit operating with one pump – I didn't really need to make precise calculations to establish that this would represent a considerable saving in energy consumption, though I estimate that it's a reduction of more than 50%."

Soft differentiators are concerned with more distant and less obvious relationships between product features and customer benefits. Making them apparent to prospects requires a pedagogic, and very specific communications approach (see Figure 1.8).

An example here can be taken from an application of the MaxMove platform (there's a full product description in Chapter Three, page 94): a major soft differentiator for this piece of equipment is the positive effects it has on the work people who

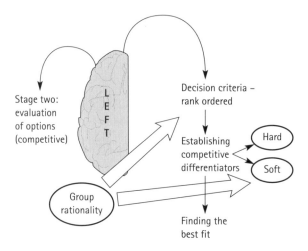

Figure 1.8 B2B purchasing

use it: because of its ease of positioning, it reduces strain injuries and, relatedly, it reduces sick leave – both of which are major – and expensive – problems in the construction industry (see the hospital construction case study, below).

Axis-pivoting platform proves itself in hospital construction

The construction of a major regional hospital in northern Europe turned out to be a proving ground for a revolutionary new type of axis-pivoting, mobile platform: as well as providing numerous advantages for the main contractor (including a reduced sick leave), a sub-contractor and the local authority who own the hospital are also now using the platform, having seen it at this site.

A major regional hospital

The hospital has 4,000 rooms on four stories, each with four meter ceiling heights; a total floor area of 88,000 sq.m; 95,000 sq.m of gypsum panel interior walls; 20,000 sq.m of ceiling panels; 7 km of ventilation pipes – a huge logistics challenge for the construction company. As part of the answer, they invested in a fleet of innovative mobile access platforms from MaxMove.

The project manager explains that the MaxMove equipment, "...was used for a large number of applications, including the mounting of wall and ceiling panels. Without MaxMove we would probably have used rolling scaffolding, where we reckon that the positioning and erection take about 20% of the total time to do the job. And of course the scaffolding has to be set up in each room separately, given that the equipment has to go through a 90 cm wide doorway opening. In the toilets, for example, which measure just 2 meters square, setup and dismantling can take longer than the panel installation. With the MaxMove equipment, however, the preparation time is minimal because it can be simply driven through 90 cm doorways and positioned within minutes."

Ergonomic benefits

The project manager sums up the advantages of the MaxMove equipment: "First, there are ergonomic advantages. It is very easy to position in all three dimensions and therefore people work at the correct height and at the best angle, with regard to their working health. This is especially important for the craft specialists such as electricians, carpenters, and the like."

Reduced sick leave

"In fact, many of the people on site found the MaxMove units actually fun to work with which makes for very good work motivation. This was indicated by the fact that sickness absence on this project was only 2%, which in my experience is very low for the construction industry in general. Many of the workers actually said to me that they would not come on our next project unless we were using the MaxMove equipment."

"Using MaxMove was definitely a factor in the success of the project," he states. "In fact its time-saving effects were definitely worth more than the cost of the equipment. Its flexibility and maneuverability meant that the logistic planning of the project became much simpler. We didn't have to worry about erecting the scaffolding or ladders and so on for the various jobs. And in the construction of interior walls it definitely saved us a lot of time and therefore made it easier to meet the project deadlines."

Clearly as a salesperson, or marketer, your ideal would be a situation where the hard differentiators of your product are obviously superior to those of its competitors, e.g. it's demonstrably faster, more powerful, has greater capacity, consumes less fuel, etc… and – best of all – costs the same or less: as pointed out above, price is the hardest of hard differentiators. In this context, Rackham makes the counter-intuitive observation that in B2B buying it's the buyers who are in a hurry (i.e. those who are being less rigorous and thorough) who tend to rely on the hard differentiators: in other words, the less you know about the technology involved, and the less willing or able you are to learn about it, the more likely you are to make your product selection on the basis of price, the hardest of hard differentiators. This is counter-intuitive in the sense that we tend to assume that a reliance on the hard facts alone is the opposite of instant, impulsive buying – as may well be the case in consumer purchasing, where a snap decision is based on soft or emotional responses to purchasing offers.

☀ A PEDAGOGIC CHALLENGE FOR B2B MARKETING

That there should be this tendency among B2B buyers represents a clear challenge for B2B marketing (analogous to that of B2C marketers' efforts to ensure that their products are perceived as "branded" products rather than commodities). This challenge is strongest where the strength of your product's market potential lies mainly in its soft differentiators. This is often the case with innovative products using new technologies. The nature of the challenge is essentially pedagogic, given that comprehending soft differentiators requires a significant amount of knowledge about how the product's features can translate into non-obvious benefits. (The book on life-cycle costing for pumps, described below, provides an example of how this pedagogic challenge can be met.)

☀ Life-cycle costing – a new book for pump purchasers

Interest is growing in the concept of life-cycle costing. However, implementing it as a real-world approach to purchasing industrial products usually requires a lot of "systems knowledge" and the capacity to convince even non-technical members of the purchasing organization. A new book applying the concept to pumps has been produced by an international co-operation among leading bodies in the pump industry.

"Life-cycle costing" (LCC) is based on the idea that the capital equipment which has the cheapest purchase price, is not always the cheapest to run and maintain. In other words, attempting to save money by buying, at the outset, on price alone can later prove to be an expensive mistake. (A closely related concept is the "total cost of ownership.") The three key elements of LCC are usually as follows: firstly, the purchase price of the equipment; secondly, the cost of the energy it consumes over its service life; and thirdly, the service and maintenance expended on it over its service life. It should be emphasized, however, that the costs arising from lost production (if failure of the product in question causes system downtime) can potentially dwarf all these other LCC cost elements. Where this is the case, it's essential to design the system to minimize these risks. Any residual value (e.g. trade-in, or second hand value) should be included, as well as a comprehensive review of how the proposed new equipment fits into the existing system, and what cost savings can be made there too.

The institutional route

Gunnar Hovstadius, Technology Director at ITT Fluid Technology and a specialist in this area explains that: "Current interest in energy efficiency dates back to the period 1994-95, when the American Department of Energy's Motor Challenge Program established contacts within the pump industry in order to explore possible improvements in pumping systems." The Department's involvement followed the passing of the Energy Policy Act, in 1992, which aimed to seek and define ways to reduce the nation's use of energy. Amongst other actions, it set minimum requirements for energy efficiency in electric motors, and allowed a five-year period for industry to comply with its requirements. A logical next step was to investigate how energy could be saved by reducing the demand from equipment driven by those electric motors, e.g. pumps.

The "bidding" model

Hovstadius points out that traditionally the purchasing of industrial equipment such as pumps follows a "bidding process" model, where manufacturers compete to provide the basic product at the lowest initial cost. "In some ways it can be argued that this has been institutionalized, for example where governments require public organizations to go to competitive tender and buy the lowest cost product. With the growing interest in LCC, there's discussion in the USA that Federal mandates to buy the lowest cost product should be complemented by a requirement to buy equipment which is in the highest 25% regarding energy efficiency. Other aspects of LCC could also be used. The idea here is not that the bidding process should disappear, but that the criteria on which it is based should be shifted toward the LCC concept."

The organizational dimension

Another element in the traditional, business to business bidding process is what can be called the "organizational dimension": very often the people responsible for buying and/or paying for the equipment are not involved in – or even responsible for – operating the equipment and paying for its operational costs. Those buying the equipment may have a fixed budget. They will probably, therefore, be less concerned with the long-term operating cost of the equipment, than completing the purchase without going over budget. Equipment is often bought by contractors who aren't going to be running the system once it's been designed and built. Consequently, there's little incentive for them to pay higher prices for more efficient equipment. In order to overcome this organizational irrationality, the future operators of the system are going to have to demand and specify optimally efficient equipment.

In an effort to escape from this sort of dysfunctionality – at least as far as the pump industry is concerned – an authoritative book has been produced. This will function as a manual for designing pump systems according to the principle of life-cycle costing. The book, some 200 pages long, has been produced in co-operation between Europump, the Hydraulic Institute in

America, and the US Department of Energy. The energy directorate of the EU has also taken an informed interest in its production, and, in addition, the vast majority of pump manufacturers participated. Hovstadius, who's been intimately involved in the book's production, states that "our point is that the concept of life-cycle costing is a much more sophisticated – and ultimately realistic – way of buying industrial products like pumps. This approach is making a breakthrough, with for example many articles appearing in the trade press. The idea with the book is to provide both practical guidance and hard data to enable all those involved in pump purchases to understand the dynamics of pump *systems* – which are the key to applying the LCC concept to pumps."

"Many of these principles and ideas around the LCC concept are fairly well understood by engineers, and the people who directly operate the equipment," says Hovstadius. "The real challenge is to bring these concepts to other people within the organization, for example, financial officers and general managers who need to be given a sense of how life-cycle costing can work in the real world. Then we can overcome the organizational divisions between those who have the purchasing budgets and those responsible for the operating costs."

Turning soft into hard differentiators

With the same aim in view, Rackham advises salespeople to pursue a strategy of turning any soft differentiators their product may possess into hard differentiators. He comments that this is what experts do: experts are people who are able to objectify, in some way or another, soft differentiators in areas where they are experts, thereby hardening them as criteria for making judgements. He suggests three methods by which salespeople can help their prospects to do this. One is to get the potential customer himself/herself to define the differentiators in question. Secondly, to refine the differentiator, i.e. to add your own ideas and comments to the customer's idea of a differentiator. And thirdly, what he calls repositioning which here means creating objective measures of soft differentiators. This approach is especially useful where other people in the organization need to be convinced, i.e. where one of the purchasers involved has been convinced by a soft differentiator but then has the task of persuading the others to share this view. Specific and rigorous research projects are one way to obtain objective measures of soft differentiators, as in the project described below.

☀ Research indicates improved aeration from horizontal flow

Recent research, carried out jointly by ITT Flygt and a national research agency indicates that creating a horizontal flow in aerobic process tanks significantly increases the efficiency of oxygen transfer. The implication of these findings is that induced horizontal flow should always be considered in the design of waste water treatment plants.

The use of aeration equipment produces a "two-phase" flow in treatment tanks: this means that two different media, in this case air and water, are flowing together. An inevitable effect of the two-phase flow is the generation of secondary spiral motions. These spiral motions have a negative effect on aeration because they increase the upward velocity of the bubbles, and therefore, reduce bubble residence time, which in turn, means that less oxygen gets transferred to the water. Consequently, anything that can be done to counter this spiraling tendency will increase oxygen transfer efficiency.

Two counter-spiral strategies

Theoretically, there are two possible ways to achieve this spiral-countering effect: one alternative would be to have total (or at least very dense) bottom coverage with diffusers. This would eliminate spiral effects simply by the density of the rising columns of air bubbles; being so close to each other, they would interfere with each other's tendency to spiral and thus prevent spirals from developing. The other solution is to generate a current across the top of the diffusers. Current generation, again, works by spiral prevention; it draws the column of bubbles off to one side of the diffuser and therefore away from the concentration of bubbles above the diffuser – which is the causative factor in spiral formation. This has the effect of decreasing the speed with which the bubbles float to the surface. So, again, current generation will prolong average bubble residence times, and consequently increase oxygen transfer efficiency.

Horizontal flow – the practical alternative

In reality, total bottom coverage is not possible and even the densest possible coverage has a number of practical drawbacks. Firstly, it's very expensive. Secondly, in order to work effectively, the diffusers would have to be configured in a perfectly even way, which could be technically difficult to achieve. Therefore, in the real world, the use of current generators is a more viable solution – though, of course, the density of the diffusers is also an important variable. Starting from this point, the research effort reported here set out to establish the optimal conditions of aeration with regard to current-generation variables (number of mixers, speed of flow, etc.) and diffuser variables (number of diffusers, configuration, etc.).

Practical experimental work was carried out at a small plant, serving a rural community. It has a circular treatment tank. This was first taken out of service and thoroughly cleaned. Ten grids of Sanitaire membrane diffusers were installed at the bottom. Two of Flygt's "banana blade" submersible mixers were installed. The aeration tests were then carried out in two phases; during the first phase clean water was used, in the second phase, waste water. For the clean water tests the tank was filled with tap water and chemicals were added to remove oxygen from the water. (These are the standard conditions for aeration efficiency tests.) Six oxygen probes, to measure oxygen transfer efficiency, were placed in the tank and the two submersible mixers were used to generate horizontal flows in the tank. Approximately 50 full-scale, individual tests were then carried out over the two-year period, testing different arrangements of the mixers, numbers and configuration of diffusers, etc. These tests were then repeated during the second, two-year phase using waste water.

Two system conditions

The first was called "constant aeration." In this condition:

- every other diffusers grid was functioning (i.e. 5 out of 10)
- the air flow to each diffuser was 2.23 m^3/hr, and
- three horizontal flow speeds were tested; 0, 0.33, and 0.46 m/s.

The second condition was called "normal functioning." In this:

- all ten of the diffusers grids were functioning
- the air flow to each diffuser was 1.33 m^3/hr, and
- four horizontal flow speeds were tested: 0, 0.17, 0.33, and 0.46 m/s.

Results

In the constant aeration state it was found that the increase in oxygen transferred between 0 velocity and a velocity of 0.35 m/s was about 40%, both for clean and for waste water. In the normal functioning state, this increase was found to be about 30% for clean water and 20% for waste water. Another interesting finding from these tests is that there appears to be a critical velocity range in terms of increasing oxygen uptake; there's not much effect from 0 to 0.15 m/s, but above this and up to approximately 0.35 m/s there is a fairly steady rise in the rate of oxygen uptake. With further increases in velocity, the rise in oxygen uptake does not rise so steeply.

Optimal system variables

A further significant finding was that the optimal point of operation, in terms of power consumption, for the combined mixer-blower system also falls around a velocity of 0.30 m/s. Fortunately, therefore, there appears to be a conjunction of efficiencies in both oxygen transfer and power consumption at around this velocity. A comparison, in terms of power consumption, with the original mechanical aerators used at the plant indicates the following: using 1 kW of power the mechanical aerators were able to transfer 1.5 kg of oxygen. The horizontal-flow-diffuser system achieved 3 kg per kW.

The practical advantages

Given the above findings, it can, therefore, be assumed that the installation of horizontal flow equipment could result in: a 50% increase in oxygen transfer, a 30% decrease in the amount of air (and number of diffusers) required, and a 15% to 25% reduction in total energy consumption for the aeration system. These, and other, advantages of installing horizontal flow generating equipment can be explained by the following practical benefits:

- the number of diffusers could be reduced
- compressor size, and consequently running costs, could be reduced
- installation of the total aeration system would be simplified
- flexibility of operation would be increased, e.g. the diffusers could be shut off without creating settling problems
- mixing conditions in the tank would be improved.

A design imperative

All of these advantages would result in reduced running costs for the aeration system. This cost saving would, of course, have to be offset against the overall cost of installing current generating equipment, i.e., the capital, installation, and the running cost of, for example, mixers. Generally, however, when applied in appropriate circumstances, these equipment costs should be more than outweighed by the running cost advantages referred to above.

Resolving concerns

During the third phase of the B2B buying process, the resolution of concerns, Rackham's strategy advice to the salesperson is to uncover concerns and resolve fears. These will always exist because, he points out, the process of judging alternatives by comparing criteria with differentiators will always involve trade-offs; consequently, there will never be a perfect match. For example, it is highly unlikely that the product which has the best performance, or the best quality will also have the lowest price. Customers, therefore, have to make trade-offs amongst their decision criteria – if they originally wanted best performance *and* lowest price, then one of these will have to be sacrificed in favour of the other. Such trade-offs can often provoke anxiety – is the higher price really going to result in better performance? One method of helping prospects to dispel such concerns is to provide them with a comparative study of your product with a competitor's, as in the mining case study overleaf.

There can be many other areas of concern, which may be less obvious for sales and marketing people. One of these can be "post-purchase justification."

Comparative performance of crushers at North American gold mine

A gold mine in North America opted for three Svedala H-6000's cone crushers, which have exceeded production targets and reduced power consumption. This was largely due to their automated adjustment. The mine first installed a cone crusher from another manufacturer for a three month trial. Somewhat later, a Svedala H-6000 cone crusher was brought to site and the two machines ran together for a short period.

The capital cost of the other manufacturer's machine was 20% more but the major factor which swung the purchasing decision, according to the crusher supervisor at the site, was the fact that the Svedala machine has automatic setting regulation (ASR). The crusher supervisor reports that, "After the initial start-up phase, it ran completely automatically whereas the other machine required manual adjustment." The other machine's need for manual adjustment was reflected in performance: although the other machine is rated at a throughput of 500 tons per hour and the Svedala is rated 400 tons per hour, the actual average per crusher was 150 tons for the rival machine and 160 tons per hour for the Svedala. In addition to this increased throughput, staff could attend to other duties instead of standing by to make machine adjustments.

Wear part replacement also showed a cost advantage for the Svedala machine. Liner life for the other machine was approximately 300 hours and replacement took longer than the Svedala liner, which had a life of 400 hours. As a bonus, the replacement parts are less costly.

Although the Svedala machine was also supposed to have been on a three month trial, in fact the decision to purchase it, plus two more of the same H-6000 machines, was made about four or five weeks after its first appearance on site. Production for a 20-hour shift is now approximately 11,500 tons, which exceeds the targeted 10,000 tons. Productivity is so good that one of the three Svedalas can normally be on standby which means that there is no downtime for maintenance. There's also been a considerable energy saving: the supervisor estimates that, "we have been saving between $45,000 and $50,000 per month since we switched to the Svedala crushers and in fact we are now running with one generator less than we did before the Svedalas were installed."

Post-purchase justification

As suggested above, B2B purchases will be meditated by the organizational ideology of rationality. What this means is that individuals within organizations will seek to present and justify their purchasing preferences to other organizational members in terms which both parties can accept as rational. This becomes especially significant in the final phase of B2B purchasing: "post-purchase justification." The need for this arises from the essentially group nature of organizational decision-making: having made a major purchasing decision, the responsible individual (or sub-group) is always faced with the task (implicitly or explicitly) of legitimizing their decision to other members of the organization – their boss, the board of directors, ultimately the owners of the organization. Decision-makers outside what Rackham calls the organization's focus of power may be fearful of having their decisions challenge by those within it. (Rackham comments that concerns of this sensitive type may often be hidden behind discussion about price. Customers who are worried about such issues may feel more comfortable focussing on the hard, and "acceptable," question of price as a way to express concerns which they may not wish to express more openly.) Given the prevailing ideology of rationality within organizations, this justification will be constructed out of rational arguments.

This can be contrasted with the post-purchase situation of an individual consumer – if you're spending your own money, you don't have to answer to anyone. Of course, there are parallel phenomena here, at the individual level, for both B2B and consumer buyers. There's the well-known phenomenon of rationalization: people tend to make decisions first and then accumulate rational justifications afterwards. A related phenomenon is cognitive dissonance and the need to reduce it. This refers to the anxiety people often experience following a major purchase: having committed to the purchase, doubt begins to set in. (This may be related to bounded rationality, i.e. we know sub-consciously that we made the decision intuitively, rather than via the exhaustive analysis which we would consciously prefer to have as a decision basis.) Individuals need to construct a rational defense against the anxious suspicion that they may have made the wrong decision. Rationalization is an internal process, where individuals construct such defenses for themselves. Cognitive dissonance reduction is a social process where another individual and/or an organization (in a post-purchase situation these roles will be played by the relevant salesperson and/or the vendor organization to whom he or she belongs) provides the anxious individual with material and/or other help to assist them in their internal rationalization process.

So much for the similarities at the individual level, but there are also differences, with regard to the ultimate consequences, between the B2B and the consumer buyer: for the consumer it's their money (possibly a large amount) that's at stake. For the B2B buyer, however, their status and position in the organization – and ultimately their job – may depend on the quality of the purchasing decisions they make. This tends to intensify the desire to construct post-decision, rational justifications amongst this class of purchaser.

Front-stage management

In organizational buying, phenomena like these can also take place at the level of the sub-group: we can label this "front-stage management" (from the work of the sociologist Irwin Goffman[5] on how groups seek to influence the public presentation of themselves). The idea here is that, where a sub-group within the organization has been responsible for a purchasing decision, they may feel a need to "manage" the presentation of this decision to the rest of the organization. For example, the real, "back-stage," reasons why the sub-group selected a particular product might have had to do with the good relationships they enjoy with the relevant salespeople. This, by itself, would not be an acceptable justification of their decision in terms of the ideology of organizational rationality. When called upon to do so, they are far more likely to "front-stage" manage the legitimization of the decision by presenting a series of benefits which will accrue to the organization from the purchase of this particular product rather than any of the alternatives considered. (I shall argue, later on, that the case study – especially in an editorial format – can play a significant role in both rationalization and front-stage management for purposes of post-purchase justification. A role, which for example, image advertising cannot play.)

SUMMARY: FROM DESCRIPTION TO PRESCRIPTION

The purpose of this first chapter has been to try and describe the B2B purchasing process, and, specifically, how it differs from the B2C process (so as not to confuse the two). The point being that this maps out the territory within which the B2B marketer must act. Armed with this map, we can now set out on our journey. How we equip ourselves should naturally be determined by our understanding of the nature of the territory – a jungle will require different equipment than a desert. As suggested at the beginning of this chapter, the most prominent feature of the landscape for the B2C marketer is the consumer, but for the B2B marketer, in his/her different territory, it's *the case*. Consequently, for survival and success in B2B territory, the most essential tool is a *case focus*. This is why, in Chapter Two, I propose the term "case-based marketing" as a predominant strategic theme for B2B marketers.

NOTES

1. McDonald, M. (1995) *Marketing plans.* Oxford: Butterworth Heinemann.
2. Lynch, J. E. (1994) 'What is marketing?' in Hart, N. (ed.) *Effective Industrial Marketing.* London: Kogan Page.
3. Powers, T. L. (1991) *Modern business marketing.* St Paul: West Publishing Company.
4. Rackham, N. (1989) *Major account sales strategy.* New York: McGraw-Hill Inc.
5. Goffman, E. (1959) *The presentation of self in everyday life.* New York: Doubleday.

chapter two

ADAPTING TO
THE B2B
PARADIGM

the "case-based" marketing method

In this chapter, I shall try to draw together the discussion about product technology and organizational decision-making presented in Chapter One. I set out on those discussions by suggesting that these two dimensions of the "B2B world" could form the boundaries of a B2B paradigm. As I also suggested, a *professional* paradigm should, in addition to defining the territory, also prescribe what practitioners should *do*. Here I shall try to answer that question.

Why a sales-based model?

Why is Rackham's *sales*-based model relevant to B2B *marketers*? Some may ask why, in a book aimed at marketers, so much space should be devoted to a *sales* theorist. There are, I believe, several cogent responses to this question. Firstly, personal selling is clearly crucial to B2B marketers, in contrast to their consumer counterparts. Secondly, as I hope I've been able to make clear in the last section, Rackham (as he emphazises himself) is very much more a researcher of the *purchasing process* rather than a conventional *sales* theorist. Thirdly, this crossing of a disciplinary boundary is hopefully a healthy example of the general trend toward the breaking down of functional silos – originally erected, and traditionally defended, to protect pseudo-professional rights to particular turfs. In B2B in particular (and maybe also more generally in marketing), with the communication technologies available today, it may be time to ask where the boundary between sales and marketing actually is and whether it's meaningful to go on defending it.

it may be time to ask where the boundary between sales and marketing actually is and whether it's meaningful to go on defending it

(I know from personal conversation that Rackham, for example, regards his current work as being as much concerned with marketing as with sales.)

Decision criteria and "meta-value"

There is another and more important answer to the question of Rackham's relevance – his concept of decision criteria. These are critical aspects of B2B transactions. Why are they so important? Because they help to explain a phenomenon which is crucial in a capitalist market economy: the willingness of customers to pay more for a product than it cost to produce. This arises because the customer sees some "extra" value, for himself or herself, in the product which can't be deduced from the costs involved in its production process. Carl Eric Linn calls this phenomenon "meta-value":

> The difference between the cost of the product and the price asked for it then hides an immaterial, intangible added value connected to the buyer's interpretation of the product and resulting from the supplier's marketing and development activities.[1]

Payment for meta-value provides the profits which drive capitalist societies. Consequently, generating meta-value has to be the overriding aim of all forms of marketing.

META-VALUE AS LOCK AND KEY

Linn links meta-value very closely with "brand," whereas Rackham hardly mentions the word. (This difference of approach reflects the discussion of the differences between consumer and B2B branding in Chapter Four.) What Rackham does suggest, however, is that B2B customers perceive meta-value when they find a product whose differentiators match their decision criteria; differentiators can be seen as a key searching for the right lock (set of decision criteria). When the customer sees that they fit together, meta-value (and hence the customer's willingness to pay a profit to the producer) are released. Meta-value for consumers may amount to no more than a sense that acquiring the product in question will enhance their life-style aspirations. For B2B purchasers, on the other hand, the organizational constraints on their decision-making pre-dispose them to perceive meta-value in terms of competence to meet their particular decision criteria. Meeting these criteria depends on product differentiation. (See, for example, the North Sea case study below, where the differentiators of submersible, as opposed to dry-mounted, mixers represented meta-value for supply boat designers.)

Submersible mixers for drilling mud – a Norwegian innovation in the North Sea

Drilling "mud" is extensively used in the oil industry. A Norwegian company has come up with the novel idea of using electric, submersible mixers to keep this material suspended during its transit on supply boats to North Sea platforms.

Drilling mud is a vital substance in the oil drilling industry. It has three functions. Firstly, it is used as a flushing material for drilling operations, to transport cuttings up from the hole and to keep the drill bit, in the bottom of the hole, clear of cuttings. Secondly, it helps to regulate the pressure emerging from an oil field. (This includes its role in trying to prevent "blow-outs".) Its principal role, however, is as a flushing material. In this context, drilling mud performs several functions: It keeps cuttings suspended while the mud is circulating, during drilling operations. When these stop, it forms a gel which prevents the cuttings falling to the bottom of the hole, until circulation is restarted, which breaks up the gel. It also provides lubrication and cooling and acts as an anti-corrosion agent.

Submersible suspension

When stored in tanks, both on the supply boats going out to the rigs and on the platforms themselves, the drilling mud has to be kept suspended, to prevent its various components sedimenting in layers by weight. Conventionally, this is achieved using dry-mounted, hydraulic agitators. Now, however, a Norwegian company has come up with the idea of using electric, submersible mixers to perform this task. There are many reasons why this solution is preferable: Firstly, the installation costs are lower. Secondly, no servicing is required for spindle-bearings. Thirdly, submersible mixers are not susceptible to contamination by the drilling mud, as is the hydraulic, dry-mounted alternative. Fourthly, submersible mixers take up less space, weigh less and consume less energy. Finally, submersibles operate noiselessly.

Marine constraints overcome conservatism

Despite the obvious advantages, there has been quite a bit of resistance to the idea of using electric submersible mixers. The oil industry tends, in any case, to be quite conservative about the equipment it uses, and hydraulic and electric, dry-mounted agitators have been used in America for this purpose for a long time. This tradition has proved quite difficult to overcome. Conventionally, dry-mounted agitators are still used on off-shore rigs, while submersibles are common on supply boats, but they are usually hydraulically driven. One reason why this submersible breakthrough has occurred in relation to boats may be the question of space. At land-based tanks, and also (to a certain extent) at tanks on platforms, there is more space available for mixers, so the space-saving feature of the submersible mixer was not really appreciated. This only really sank in when it came to tanks on boats, where space is very much at a premium.

Enormous, potential market

This application represents a very large potential market for submersible mixers. In Norway alone, each of the approximately 120 North Sea supply boats would require about six mixers for its drilling mud storage tanks. If submersibles were used in the tanks on the rigs, between 15 and 25 mixers would be required for each rig and there are a total of about 48 rigs in the Norwegian section of the North Sea alone. In addition, "stand-by" ships, which are required by law to be moored next to platforms in case of emergency situations, are also equipped with drilling mud tanks. These vessels are utilized as extra storage capacity by the rigs, as for example in the storing of drilling mud. Their mud tanks could also benefit from conversion to submersible mixing. The same could, indeed, be said of drilling mud suspension operations all over the world – both onshore and offshore.

Rackham observes that while he is referring to the sort of differentiation which can be directly controlled by salespeople, the concept of competitive differentiation itself was originally developed in marketing: "the objective of competitive differentiation is to make your product distinct in the customer's mind from other available alternatives."[2] In marketing terms, differentiation starts with product design, then continues through activities like pricing, promotion, and advertising strategy. Unfortunately, he says, most marketers lose interest at this point: "When the product is designed, priced, and promoted, then marketing has done its work. But it's exactly at this juncture – when the product is ready to be sold to customers – that differentiation becomes even more important." This is where salespeople take over the process of differentiation in interaction with the individual customer.

Differentiation – "Macro" and "Micro"

Rackham introduces the term "micro-differentiation" to distinguish what salespeople are doing from "macro-differentiation," which is what marketing people do through activities such as pricing and advertising. Macro-differentiation is aimed at the whole market, or a particular segment, it doesn't come down to the level of the individual customer. Advertising, for example,

> 66 will differentiate the product by emphasising those areas where the product is strong and which *are likely to have the most impact on the majority of the buying population of the target market.* If you have the good fortune to be in a market where all customers behave in precisely the same way, and where what's important to one customer is likely to be equally important to another, then your advertising would have an equally powerful differentiating effect on each customer. But, inevitably, customers differ. It is quite possible that the differentiator which has the most effect on one customer may be unimportant to another. 99 [3]

He goes on to say that the classic marketing tools of advertising and promotion, "can give overall positioning to a product, but they can't come down to the level of the individual customer."[4]

Case stories as "market reaction" research

There is, however, an exception to this claim – the classic promotional tool of the *case story*; by definition, this is based on the individual customer. Later we'll be looking at how case stories can be effectively used in marketing communications, but here we can consider their potential role in B2B marketing in general. Their relevance to this discussion is that a properly recorded case story should reveal both the customer's decision criteria and how the product's differentiators were able to fulfil these – or failed to do so. This negative alternative alerts us to the reality that the term case story is not limited to accounts of successful sales which are written up and publicized for promotional purposes: in principle, every sales process conducted by the company is a case story – even where the sale was unsuccessful. Even case stories in this sense should reveal decision criteria, and, where the sale was unsuccessful, why the product's differentiator's failed to meet them. From a marketing point of view this information is just as important. In summary, case stories, in this wider sense are an invaluable source of marketing information – a very effective form of market reaction research. Very effective because, as Rackham points out, criteria arise or evolve during the sales process which is often prolonged and has many stages. In effect prospects "discover" or formulate decision criteria together with the salesperson. Consequently, this type of market information cannot really be researched by conventional methods, such as opinion surveys, focus groups, etc.

The longevity of decision criteria

Rackham stresses longevity as an additional relevance of decision criteria. They are not only the key to perceived meta-value in the "one-off" sale, they also tend to live on in the customer's mind, influencing sale after sale. Decision criteria may be developed during one particular sales process but once customers have evolved a

decision criteria tend to live on in the customer's mind, influencing sale after sale – a micro-world view for a particular product set of criteria for purchasing a particular type of product, they are likely to use the same criteria when purchasing a similar type of product in the future. In effect, they become part of the customer's way of structuring their business and purchasing realities – a micro-world view for a particular product area. This "specific-product-world-view" will comprise both a set of beliefs about what is important in judging products of this type and also a loyalty to one, or a few, companies who are perceived to be capable of providing quality in this product area. In marketing terms, the ideal situation is clearly to influence prospects' decision criteria in such a way that a structural bias in favor of your company is built into their habitual pattern of thinking about the relevant product area. (This is the most importance aspect of B2B branding (see Chapter Four).)

To re-cap, the purpose of differentiation, in both marketing (macro) and sales (micro), is to make a product, or more accurately a product package (i.e. the features of the product plus its price, delivery terms, after-sales service, means of payment, etc.), as attractive to as many prospective customers as possible. Ideally, differentiation achieves this by providing a "key" that perfectly fits the "lock" of each prospect's *decision criteria*. The objective of marketing is to provide a product with a master key, i.e. one that will fit the decision criteria of every prospect (or more realistically, as many as possible) in its target market. Salespeople use differentiation on an individual level to forge a unique key for each prospect, in response to what they learn about that particular prospect's decision criteria. What can be suggested here is that there is something between a master key and a unique key. This something-in-between can be discovered by *generalizing* from individual sales cases.

Mastering decision criteria

Given this, one of the major objectives for B2B marketers must be to master the decision criteria used by customers and prospects in relation to each of the particular types of products they are engaged in marketing. (Mastering here means having analyzed enough case material to fully understand the patterns and trends in the relevant decision criteria.) This mastering of decision criteria can usefully be seen as one half of the B2B marketer's job (the other half being brand building, centered around the projection of competence, as described in Chapter Four, page 107.) Ultimately, these two sides of B2B marketing interact with each other, in the sense that competence-brand-building can be seen as the *strategy*, while mastering decision criteria represents the *tactics*, i.e. the more completely a company can fulfil the specific requirements of its particular customers, the more firmly based will its reputation for technical competence become. This approach, of attempting to integrate actual decision criteria with brand building, can be called a case-based approach to B2B marketing.

Case-based marketing for B2B

This approach to marketing incorporates both macro and micro, as per the discussion of Rackham's model above. The idea is that B2B *marketers* (as well as sales-people) can learn from individual cases. An analogy can be drawn here with especially the legal but also the medical professions, in both of which competence is taught and acquired via a case-based approach. In contrast, the role of the consumer marketer could be compared to that of a politician or entertainer; i.e. (in order to succeed) their task is to appeal to (and/or influence or create) universal values. These are universal in the sense that they are designed to appeal to as many people as possible in the target group, which in the case of a politician is the voting population of the political territory in which they are standing, or in the case of the entertainer (or consumer marketer) a target market based on demographics or life style. The attractive values of the politician/entertainer do not (in any tightly defined sense) have to work. All that's necessary for success is that they are persuasive enough to elicit a favorable response from a majority (or at least a large enough number) of the individuals in the targeted group.

To extend the lock-and-key metaphor introduced above, the politician/entertainer's key to meta-value is a master key – it has to fit many locks. While these might be simple, they tend to change rapidly and unpredictably. Espousing the right values and projecting the right image is, as many politicians, entertainers, and consumer marketers have discovered, an inexact science – despite the focus group and other contemporary opinion research. "A week is a long time in politics" (and entertainment). What's fashionable this week may not be next week.

The demands that B2B marketers need to meet are less fickle but more rigorous. Decision criteria often require technical solutions which have to work in practice as well as theory. As we saw, Rackham states that the salesperson's job is to uncover, influence, and maximize the perceived fit between his/her product's differentiators and the prospect's decision criteria. How does a B2B *marketer* master the relevant decision criteria? There are at least two problems here:

- research (because to repeat Rackham's point about the emergence of criteria; they "arise" or evolve during the sales process so they cannot be effectively researched by conventional methods, such as opinion surveys, focus groups, etc.)

- numbers (sales people deal with prospects one at a time, whereas marketers have to deal with the whole potential market. A salesperson will be presented with a manageable number of criteria, whereas the number for the marketer is potentially much larger).

We've already touched on the solution to problem one – the sales case story. There are, of course, a number of provisos; the company's salespeople have to be both aware of, and diligent in their task of uncovering and recording, prospect's decision criteria. Secondly, there have to be mechanisms for collecting and assessing these criteria. These should provide B2B marketers with a systematic collection of decision criteria for each product and product area for which they are responsible, including a rank ordering of the criteria.

This will provide a population of customer decision criteria for marketing analysis, which brings us on to problem two. Rackham stresses the uniqueness of each customer's set of decision criteria, and doubtless there is an ultimate truth in this. On the other hand, all marketing involves a tension between satisfying an individual customer and generating a profit for the company, as many theorists have pointed out (e.g. Hugh Davidson[5]). From the customer satisfaction point of view, segments of one individual might be the ideal, but going through the process of new product development for a single customer is (with the exception of governments and the super rich) unlikely to prove profitable. Consequently, marketing must approach customers *en masse*.

Trends and patterns

Given this, rather than trying to respond to the decision criteria of each and every prospect (as a salesperson should) the marketer can analyze the population of criteria available in order to establish the patterns and trends reflected in them. (Depending on the size and complexity of the material, this analysis could range in technique from simply reading through salespeople's reports and forming subjective impressions, to complete statistical analysis, with decision criteria weighted according to customer's rank ordering.) To invoke a medical analogy, this could be compared with a district medical officer going through the case notes of all the doctors in his or her area. Although each case is unique, what he or she can learn from this are the general patterns and trends in the health of the population in his or her district – are people living longer? Are they more or less fertile than previously? Is there any evidence of epidemics? Can specific sources for food poisoning or allergies be identified?

It can be assumed that patterns and trends in decision criteria will exist in all markets. At the most obvious level, a general striving for efficiency among industrial customers can be anticipated, though interestingly, subtle differences of definition can be identified; for example, is the cost-value trade-off conceptualized simply in terms of the one-off purchase price of a product or are the total costs of ownership, i.e. the product's life-cycle costs being considered? (See page 38.) In some markets other, more recent and nuanced trends will be found; for example, in some countries environmental and health and safety considerations may rank very high as decision criteria.

The results of these analyses can, first of all, be fed into the process of product development. Their value here is enhanced by the fact that these criteria have emerged from prolonged and rigorous thinking by customers during an actual sale process, rather than their perhaps superficial responses to questionnaire-type research. Secondly, identifying the pattern and trends in customers' decision criteria provides an ideal basis for formulating marketing communication objectives: where your products have been successful in satisfying prevailing criteria, this can be specifically published for the reference of existing and future prospects. Where your products have failed, they can (where possible) be modified accordingly, or appropriately replaced. These new products can then be publicized, stressing how they now meet the relevant criteria. This process introduces extremely valuable post-launch feed-back mechanisms into the more conventional marketing process, see Figure 2.1.

Mao Tse Tung –

"what we learn from the people or randomly

we can teach to them

systematically"

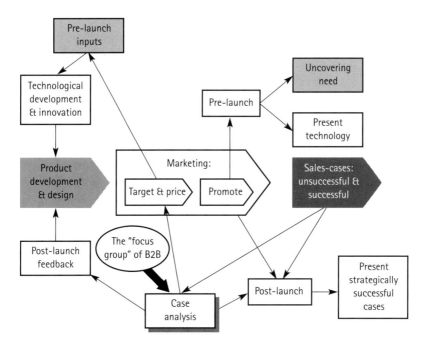

Figure 2.1 Case-based marketing for B2B

In this way case analysis can act as the focus group of B2B marketing, enabling its practitioners to fulfil the prescription of Mao Tse Tung who once said, "what we learn from the people randomly we can teach to them systematically." (While objectively a disaster as a political leader, Mao was certainly a good marketer of himself and the Chinese Communist Party, which he dominated. Interestingly, in the context of this book, he clearly considered himself to be engaged in B2B marketing. In reality, the feedback channels essential for real B2B marketing had, in the China of his time, been brutally severed by political repression. What he was actually doing was much more like B2C marketing – whipping up mass self-expressive enthusiasm for his own ideological fashion preferences, though the consequences of his bad taste were infinitely more tragic than anything that can be laid at the door of more conventional B2C marketers.)

Summarizing case-based marketing – the B2B paradigm

The basic process flow of case-based marketing can be seen in Figure 2.1. Essentially, it adds a number of additional, post-launch feedback loops to a more conventional model of the marketing process. The process starts with product development and design. (Though, in the B2B world, where products are continually adapted and adjusted – even for particular customers – it could be argued that the process is much more like an ongoing cycle.) There is input at this pre-launch stage from both technological development and innovation and from the marketing processes of targeting and pricing. When a final product package design has been arrived at, the conventional marketing process can move onto promotion, which at this pre-launch or launch stage will concentrate on uncovering the need and presenting the technology which is being offered to fulfil it.

As the sales force takes over the new product, the post-launch mechanisms of case-based marketing can start to function. This is perhaps the greatest moment of truth in the entire business process – when the salesperson presents, face-to-face, the new product to the first potential customer. How is he or she going to react? This is no longer a matter of deductions from statistics – it's a concrete, existential event. The information which the sales force can garner from these encounters, can claim a higher level of reality than any other source of marketing information. Because of the depth of effort that B2B purchasers commonly put into formulating their decision criteria, its analysis can provide a much more reliable measure of market reaction than can the (inevitably) off-the-top-of-the-head responses of a focus group.

The fruits of such case analysis can provide post-launch feedback into the product development and design process and also into the targeting and pricing process, which may, as a result of this feedback, need to be re-aligned. Case analysis should also, of course, be used to guide further promotional activities, which for B2B products, should also be *case-based*. (The details of how this can be done will be set out in Chapter Seven.)

It might be suggested that this, rather than being a dramatic example of paradigm revelation, is merely the everyday practice of most B2B companies, and, indeed, in my experience, established B2B practitioners (at least the more successful ones) do tend to be very case-oriented. Nonetheless, I do see a value in "theorizing" such practice for several reasons:

- placing it in the context of a complete theoretical paradigm can make it more systematically applied in practice – less reliant on the vagaries of intuition

- it can provide the core (as suggested above) for a more focussed and distinct professional identity for B2B marketers, and consequently enhance their self-image, motivation, and self-conscious professional skills.

Further elements of the B2B paradigm

In addition to procedural description, it is useful to elaborate on a number of elements of the paradigm which have emerged from this discussion; namely, the role of rationality, the "science-art" cultural divide and the professional analogies: lawyer vs entertainer.

☀ THE ROLE OF RATIONALITY – PERFECT RATIONALITY OR "RATIONAL DISCOURSE"

Given the complexity of the B2B purchasing process, outlined above, it's clear that rationality is going to play a more necessary role than is the case in consumer purchasing. This does not, however, imply that B2B buying is an *entirely* rational process (indeed, it's doubtful whether any form of human behavior can be reduced to entirely rational processes). One obvious phenomenon working against this is "bounded rationality." This, simply, is the idea that no organization, or group or individual within an organization, has the resources (in terms of time, energy, money, and brain capacity) to look at all the possibly relevant information about all the competitive alternatives available – as complete rationality would require.

What happens in the real world is that, at some point (which may vary between individual decision-makers) in the evaluation process, the decision-makers will determine that they have considered enough information to be able to make a decision. What this means, essentially, is that they decide to make a leap of faith from the top of a heap of evidence. This may vary in height from case to case, but it will never be high enough to *guarantee* a safe landing on the side of certainty.

Another way of expressing this is to introduce the concept of rational discourse. I'm *not* arguing the crude case that B2B transactions are rational while B2C are emotional. Rather than the blunt word rational, I'd like to suggest the more nuanced idea that "B2B transactions are conducted within a context of rational discourse" (even if the discourse is limited to one salesperson and one organizational buyer – though for any significant B2B purchase, this would be an unusually circumscribed cast of characters). Applying the term rational discourse to the process requires (or at least implies) adherence to the following implicit rules:

- the arguments used are explicitly formulated, both when presented verbally and in writing

- these arguments will be based (at least in part) on previously acquired and publicly available knowledge and experience

- there is an expectation that arguments will either be accepted or challenged also on the basis of previously acquired and publicly available knowledge and experience

- there is an implicit agreement that quantifiable and/or publicly demonstrable evidence should count more heavily in resolving disagreements than subjective value judgements or emotional insights

(These rules can be compared with the rules of evidence in legal proceedings.)

The case study below is an example of this type of rational discourse, where supercritical water oxidation is present and compared with a rival waste disposal technique, wet air oxidation.

Supercritical water oxidation – the environmental answer to organic waste disposal?

Environmentally benign waste disposal is becoming a more acute problem. A newly developed process, supercritical water oxidation is demonstrating extremely efficient organic waste destruction (99.99%) plus excellent environmental characteristics (none of the emissions associated with incineration). The process is especially suitable for the treatment of waste water and sludge from domestic sewage and the paper and pharmaceutical industries.

Supercritical water

Water enters a special condition, or "fourth phase", in addition to the familiar solid, liquid, and gaseous phases, when its temperature and pressure are above 374°C and 221 bar. In this region, its properties change, density being less than that of the liquid, viscosity the same as the gas, and diffusivity about mid-way between the liquid and the gas. Most importantly, the solubility of gases and organic compounds are increased to almost 100% while inorganic compounds become almost insoluble.

These special properties have been known theoretically for a long time and in the 1970s and 1980s work began on exploiting them for practical applications. An oxygen supply was introduced and the process is now know as Supercritical Water Oxidation (SCWO). With organic molecules and the added oxygen fully dissolved, a uniform homogeneous mixture is created and reactions can proceed at the intrinsic rate, i.e., the theoretically maximum rate for chemical reactions. Consequently, residence time in the reactor is only about one minute. Despite this brief residence, the method achieves a 99.99% destruction of organic contaminants.

Complete oxidation

Burning is also an oxidation process but suffers from several disadvantages, one of which is incomplete combustion and the consequent need to scrub the stack gases to rid them of environmentally dangerous compounds such as dioxins. SCWO results in complete destruction irrespective of the feed entering the process, even PCBs. Due to the lower reaction temperatures, the harmful oxides of nitrogen are not formed; these are toxic and acidic and can cause eutrophication (algal blooms) in fresh water.

Benign output

Unlike incineration, SCWO is a totally enclosed process and the reaction products are discharged at very close to atmospheric pressures and temperatures. Furthermore, they are benign, consisting mainly of CO_2, water, and nitrogen. These substances do not need expensive scrubbing to make them suitable for discharge to the environment. Organic and inorganic halogens are converted to the corresponding acids and organic and inorganic sulphur are converted to sulphuric acid. These are far easier to deal with in liquid form than as gases like sulphur dioxide which causes acid rain. Heavy metals are oxidized to their highest oxidation state and are separated together with any inert materials as a fine, non-leachable ash which can be used much like power station ash for landscaping, aggregates, and similar applications.

Heat economy

Both SCWO and incineration are auto-thermal, or self-sustaining, once the process is up to operating temperature. However, they both need sufficient organic material in the feed stock or external heating must be applied;

incineration needs well in excess of 25% before becoming auto thermal whereas SCWO can be auto thermal with only 3–4% of organic material in the feed. The SCWO process can therefore show considerable primary fuel savings when compared with incineration.

"Wet air" comparison

The SCWO process has similarities to wet air oxidation which is in use in a number of plants already. However, the wet air process operates at temperatures of up to 300°C and 200 bar (depending on the process). This is below the critical point of water and typically achieves only 70% destruction of organic carbon, even with residence times in the reactor of up to six hours. Such long residence times require much larger reactors, typically 100 times larger than those required for supercritical processing.

Safety issues

Nevertheless, Chematur's Development Director, Lars Stenmark suggests that, "the wet air process may have paved the way for SCWO: people in industries which normally use unstressed equipment have a psychological barrier which makes them wary of high temperatures and pressures. In fact, compared with many modern pressure vessels, the SCWO process uses very modest pressures and temperatures – the pressures are no higher than those in common gas bottles found in workshops world wide and the reactors are not much larger."

Under normal operating conditions, both systems are completely safe. Aqua Critox plants have modern interlocks so that in the event of pressure drop or other malfunction, the plant shuts down. However, there can always be catastrophic accidents, like a crane dropping a load or, in some parts of the world, terrorist attack. With a reactor burst under these circumstances, the smaller unit would cause less damage, even though the contents flashed into steam, than the larger reactor. If toxic waste were being processed, the smaller vessel, containing only about 5% toxic material, would contain less than the larger one.

The salt limitation

Other problems sometimes associated with SCWO are salt deposits and corrosion. Lars Stenmark claims that, "these are also more manageable than may be commonly thought." Soluble salts in a few flows become insoluble under supercritical conditions and this can lead to scaling of the heat exchanger walls. Obviously, wherever possible it is advisable to avoid dealing with flows which contain high salt saturations. Meanwhile the possibility of pre-treating flows to remove salts is being investigated as well as adapting the process so that higher salt concentrations are not a problem. In fact, scaling is minimal for slurries which contain inert materials because suspended particles act as nuclei for salt precipitation before the fluid reaches the walls of the heat exchanger. Additionally, these inert materials can also scour the walls and pipe work, acting as an abrasive cleaner to remove salt deposits. One of the most important applications, domestic sewage, normally contains considerably less than 1% salt and so does not cause a problem.

Corrosion

Halogens and hydrochloric acids for example can be highly corrosive, especially at high temperatures. "The Forschungszentrum in Karlsruhe did studies on corrosion in super critical water during the 1990s and discovered that no corrosion takes place at temperatures above 380°C because there is no dissociation above that temperature." The problem is in the transitional stage from 300° to about 370° and therefore the vulnerable part of the process is the heat exchanger where the flow is raised to this temperature. There is no corrosion in the reactor itself. Chematur has developed proprietary methods to overcome this corrosion problem in the heat exchanger.

In addition, these characteristics of rational discourse also neatly link it together with the two metaphors for B2B marketing which I want to invoke namely: the conduct of the natural sciences and the proceedings of the legal profession. Both of these might be said to progress via rational discourse, in the sense outlined above.

The cultural divide – science vs art

In making the analogy (as in Chapter One) between, B2B-technology-formal-organization and Science and B2C-fashion-life-style-aspirations and Art, we are reflecting a very profound cultural divide within western society. This is the state of affairs that C. P. Snow famously characterized as "the two cultures." More recently, Richard Tarnas, in his book *The Passion of the Western Mind*, has traced the historical roots of this split in western culture.

> From the complex matrix of the Renaissance had issued forth two distinct streams of culture, two temperaments or general approaches to human existence characteristic of the Western mind. One emerged in the Scientific Revolution and Enlightenment and stressed rationality, empirical science, and skeptical secularism. The other was its polar complement, sharing common roots in the Renaissance and classical Greco-Roman culture (and in the Reformation as well), but tending to express just those aspects of human experience suppressed by the Enlightenment's overriding spirit of rationalism. [6]

As we can see, this division in marketing rests on a very deep and long-established separation between two very different spheres of human activity: on the one hand, systematic research aimed at understanding and controlling processes in the natural world and, on the other, the pursuit of beauty and the "good life" (and perhaps other humanistic values) through endeavors in all the various fields of artistic expression. England in particular embodies this dichotomy in the structure of its educational system and the composition of its cultural networks. The sciences and the arts tend to exist in separate worlds with little fruitful communication between them. Returning to our discussion of the bicameral brain, it's possible that this dichotomy may be hard-wired. From this perspective, it's hardly surprising that such a profound cultural (and possibly genetic) division of activities should "re-emerge" in a new profession such as marketing.

A misallocation of marketing skills

If we look, however, at the relatively short historical development of marketing from this perspective, it's clear that the artistic fashion side of the profession developed first and remains the dominant professional paradigm. This type of marketing was (and still is) very much concerned with the use of advertising, and other mass

"lawyer-technology-marketers," are trying to solve very well-defined (often quantifiable) problems presented by their prospects and, **given competition,** they are doing this (just like lawyers) in an adversarial context

communication techniques, to promote the sale of fast moving consumer goods. Consequently, the skills associated with these types of activity, such as creative flare, imagination, and an empathetic intuition for social and fashion trends came to predominate. When marketing was, belatedly, applied to B2B products, it was (and often still is) the case that these sorts of skill were unthinkingly imported into this very different form of marketing.

THE PROFESSIONAL ANALOGIES – LAWYER VS ENTERTAINER

In Chapter One we invoked the "lawyer-entertainer" analogy to illustrate the differences between B2B and B2C marketing. A starting point here is the assertion that marketing efforts on behalf of fashion-life-style-aspiration products can be characterized as "tele-persuading" (i.e. exercising persuasion at a distance). The analogy rests on the idea that this is very much the same as what an entertainer (or politician) does, i.e. they try to discover what their target segment of "customers" likes and then try to persuade them that their songs (policies or whatever) contain lots of it. While doing this, the B2C-marketer-entertainer-politician tries to cultivate a pleasant context by assuring the customer that, " 'we' (i.e. the company they represent) are 'good' people just like you." (For "good" read: "successful," "healthy," "respectable," "stylish," etc. according to message and target segment.)

"Lawyer-technology-marketers" are engaged in a very different kind of activity: they are trying to solve very well-defined (often quantifiable) problems presented by their prospects and, given competition, they are doing this (just like lawyers) in an adversarial context. Just like lawyers, the prospects' problems can be reduced to one question (as can the jury-person's); i.e. "who's right and who's wrong?," "who's lying and who's telling the truth?," "who should I find for?," or "who should I buy from?" Again, like lawyers, technology-marketers operate in a wider ethical context than the simple serving of their clients' self-interest: for lawyers this is the pursuit of truth and justice through the legal system. For technology-marketers this is the promotion of technological progress through the market economy.

If a lawyer gets up in court and professes her client to be innocent while, at the same time, believing this to be untrue, she is breaking the ethical code of her profession. While the situation may seldom be so clear cut for the technology-marketer, there is a parallel: the idea here is that the Anglo-Saxon legal system uses adversarial debate, guided by the rules of evidence, to arrive at the truth. (Of course, other national legal systems may put less stress on adversarial debate, but all legal systems, which are uncorrupt and free of coercive political interference, attempt to establish the truth of the matters formally brought before them via some form of the rules of evidence, i.e. they engage in rational discourse.)

A free-market economy encourages competition in marketing communications to enable customers to determine which companies have the technological lead. Here again, however, there are (at least implicitly) "rules of evidence," i.e. marketing communications in the B2B world *should* predominantly consist of the factual, ideally quantifiable, benefits to be derived from the technology being promoted. Where the techniques of fashion-marketing are applied – and prove effective – in B2B marketing, they distort, under mine, or at least hamper this socially useful purpose.

This is not to imply that the misallocation of B2C skills into B2B marketing is the consequence of any malign or conspiratorial development. As argued above, I believe that this outcome has resulted from a combination of confusing very different types of human activity and the historical preeminence of consumer-marketing – in effect, it came to be seen as "marketing" per se and when B2B manufacturers finally began to see a need for marketing, they simply imported concepts, ideas, and people from the consumer end of the spectrum. What's required now is to realize that this has been a misapplication of skills: the skills required – and even the ethical contexts – for B2B marketing are distinct and different.

☀ SUMMARY: A CULTURAL DIVIDE, PLUS A "HAND-WIRED" DIFFERENCE?

To summarize the arguments of the first two chapters, I'm suggesting that, because of both differences in the nature of their products and their patterns of customer decision-making, B2B and B2C fall on either side of one of the major fault lines in western culture; namely that between science and art: B2B resembles scientific endeavor in the sense that it frequently involves groups of people co-operating to solve specific, often quantifiable, technical problems. Whereas B2C, like art is concerned with trying to influence other people regarding such questions as "what is beautiful?" and "what is necessary for a person to live a good life?" When it comes to customer decision-making, I'm going to suggest that these differences may go even deeper than culture: they may, in fact, be hard-wired into the human brain itself in the form of the functional division of labor between the left and right hemispheres. The professional analogies I'm using to illustrate these differences are: legal/medical for B2B versus politician/entertainer for B2C.

From theory to practice

Our objective in Chapter One was to identify the boundaries and explore the territory of the B2B paradigm. In this chapter we've discussed the equipment and strategies necessary for entering, surviving, and prospering in this territory. Chapter Three looks at three practical examples of how B2B marketers have set about the task of developing and launching new products. All of them have employed (explicitly or implicitly) a case-based approach.

NOTES

1. Linn, C. E. (1998) *Brand dynamics.* Novcross, Georgia, USA: The Institute for Brand Leadership, p. 29.
2. Rackham, N. (1989) *Major account sales strategy.* New York: McGraw-Hill Inc.
3. Ibid, p. 85.
4. Ibid, p. 85.
5. Davidson, H. (1987) *Offensive marketing.* Harmondsworth: Penguin.
6. Tarnas, R. (1991) *The passion of the western mind.* London: Pimlico.

CASE-BASED STRATEGIES FOR NEW PRODUCTS

This chapter illustrates the theory which has been articulated in Chapters One and Two. The idea is not to present conventional-type "strategy analyses," with analysis of target market segments, quantifiable objectives, etc., but rather to concentrate on how a *case focus* has influenced the formulation of these strategies. This chapter presents three examples of case-based strategies:

● ITT Flygt's introduction of the submersible mixer

● Ericsson's marketing of the wireless communication module, and

● the story of a much smaller company (MaxMove) and its promotion of its innovative access platform.

In the case of ITT, the product itself was developed via a randomly discovered application case and an early market in fish farming emerged from customer initiatives. Once Flygt had decided to systematically market the submersible mixer, it set about acquiring application-specific knowledge, via laboratory research, field trials, and feed back from early customers. It then promoted its knowledge by placing case stories in the relevant trade press. The Ericsson product is so new that potential customers simply don't know how to organize their supply chains in order to maximize its benefits nor what sort of financial impact it can have on their businesses. To overcome this, Ericsson have created "ideal typical" cases for particular business areas. (We use those they've devised for the vending machine industry.) MaxMove's problem was that their product had initially been launched into a niche in the construction industry that was just too narrow (mainly because that was the background of the product's inventor). Their current strategy is to move into higher profit areas, such as aviation and manufacturing, by thoroughly analyzing each potential case application with the customer. Rather than simply supplying a piece of equipment, they can provide total "mobility-productivity solutions," each tailored to a particular case. What all three examples have in common is a sharp case focus and a reliance on intimate knowledge of particular applications.

CASE ONE: DEVELOPING AND MARKETING THE SUBMERSIBLE MIXER

A product development engineer at ITT Flygt stumbled across a farming application. By stubbornly applying a "dirty-hands-on" approach to this and other early cases, he developed the submersible mixer. Soon after this, a new marketing director at Flygt developed a plan for selling these mixers. This called for the company to systematically develop the know-how necessary to apply this unique product in different business areas. The submersible mixer now accounts for 5% of Flygt's global turnover, which was $609 million in 2000.

In 1977, ITT Flygt introduced the world's first submersible mixer. It has significant advantages over conventional, dry-mounted mixers: it's easier and quicker to install; the fact that submersible mixers are simply lowered into place means a saving on space around the tank and a minimum of construction work. Installation is measured in hours not weeks, and costs are lower. Moreover, long overhangs on the propeller shafts, a common weakness in conventional mixers, are eliminated, reducing stress and vibration. This means greater reliability and efficiency. Added to that, a submersible mixer can be rapidly raised or lowered for maintenance at any time without draining the tank, and a substitute mixer can be quickly installed as a back up. In addition, submersible mixers are noiseless, since the motor's sound is insulated by the fluid around it.

Radically different mixing

Mixing in shallow tanks was an obvious application for this new breed of mixers. Horizontal installations of conventional mixers in shallow tanks pose major difficulties: either the propeller is too close to the tank wall or the shaft is too long to be reliable and efficient. Angling the shaft poses still more difficulties. Vertically installed mixers also have problems, in particular, the fact that they generate only local mixing patterns. In contrast, a compact submersible mixer can be installed from above and yet create a horizontal, axial flow (see Figures 3.1 and 3.2). But the greatest advantage of submersible over conventional technology applies to mixing in deep, long, narrow, or any other shape vessel. That advantage is the radically different approach to mixing that submersible mixers make possible. By using readily definable and controllable forces acting on the fluid, this approach brings a new control and predictability to systems design and to specifying the hydrodynamic requirements of an installation. The result is more efficient and cost-effective systems whose final performance can be determined accurately even at the initial design stage.

The man behind the development of the submersible mixer was Hjalmar Fries, who was trained as a design engineer and from the 1960s worked with both marketing and product development for ITT Flygt. Early in his career he was involved in conducting trials of a new waste water pump designed for municipal treatment plants. The trials were being carried out in a tank located in a farming area, close to ITT Flygt's factory in Lindås, southern Sweden.

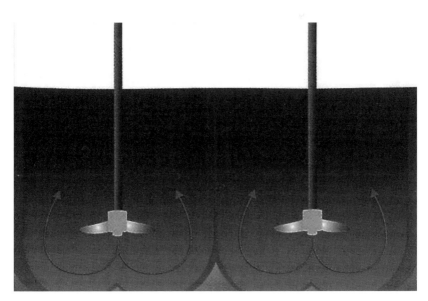

Figure 3.1 Two vertically installed mixers with dry-mounted motors

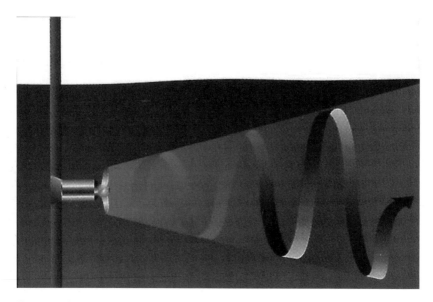

Figure 3.2 A single submersible mixer with motor incorporated into the unit

The farm market?

A local farmer suggested to Hjalmar that the pump might be used for handling the manure that his dairy cows produced. The manure was discharged into a thousand-cubic-meter tank. It then had to be removed from the tank so that the farmer could spread it over his land to fertilize the crops he grew. This casual suggestion got Hjalmar thinking about farmers as a potential market. He started asking people in the Flygt Group about farmers and discovered a culture of negativity in this area. For example, the then head of Flygt's British company told Hjalmar that he had forbidden his salespeople to visit farmers because: "(a) Flygt pumps can't deal with straw and (b) farmers are bad payers." Other people in the group either knew nothing about farmers and farming or made the comment that: farmers are not engineers and have completely different supply channels, of which Flygt has had no experience.

Hjalmar was undeterred by all this. He set up a trial to pump the dairy farm's manure. (As he points out, this is testimony to the enormous degree of personal freedom which product developers enjoyed in the company at that time.) Hjalmar emphasizes that he neither carried out, planned, nor consulted any kind of "market research" on this topic. He comments that,

> success in marketing is often about finding out things that are not necessarily logical. Taking this, maybe naïve, approach can sometimes lead to the discovery of

'the big need' in a particular area of application – as it did in this case. You can't uncover this just by getting people to answer questionnaires. To understand the reality of an equipment application area, you have to confront your product with the actual conditions of the application, observe the results and engage in dialogue about them with the end-user. ❞

Hjalmar installed a pump and some other equipment in a tank of farm manure. "It was a much bigger challenge than domestic sewage – farm manure gets a lot more contaminated with stuff like straw, bits of wood, and everything imaginable from chains to bits of farm machinery. And, sure enough the pump got blocked." Being an enthusiastic product developer, Hjalmar did not abandon the project. He and his team developed an impeller which could cut through the straw and other debris, which would otherwise clog the pump. (This was an early version of Flygt's "NevaClog" pump.)

Using complaints

Twenty of these prototype "manure" pumps were sold to farmers in Scandinavia. "Nearly all of them came back with complaints," Hjalmar recalls. "This is a crucial stage in new product development and there are two potential responses to it: the first is what I'd call the 'conventional response'. Essentially, this interprets the situation as an alarm signal for the company and its reputation and because marketing people tend not to have had much technical training, they often tend to react very defensively – given that they don't personally know how to solve any of the problems that are being reported. Consequently, their first reaction is to withdraw the products, compensate the customers, and abandon the development."

"The alternative, and more positive, reaction (which can be called the "case-based" approach) is to send the product designers *to look at* the customer's problem. In this case, this meant going to each farm and spending at least half a day there – being introduced to the farmer's wife and animals, taking coffee or beer with him, etc. This is what I mean by *looking* at a problem – and, as I had influence in the marketing department and my own budget, I was able to do this. Almost invariably, you discover that the problem is not what you expected – and the solution fairly obvious: in the case of the manure pump failures, I climbed into the tanks and stood on it! The problem was a lack of adequate mixing. The pumps were pumping out the liquids and leaving the solids behind."

Addressing mixing

Hjalmar now became very interested in the problems of mixing, particularly with regard to manure. He employed an agricultural engineer to help with this research. "We realized that efficient mixing could offer two enormous benefits to farmers: firstly, they would be able to maximize the use of the manure produced on their own farm – in some cases I discovered that farmers were only able to use a third of the volumes in their tanks. Increasing this useable volume would represent a considerable cost saving in replacing bought-in fertilizers. Secondly, effective mixing would greatly improve the fertilizing quality of manure: the solid part is carbon-rich while the liquid is rich in nitrogen. The ideal fertilizer is a balanced mix of both."

As a result of these case visits Hjalmar and his team went on to develop the submersible mixer, which now represents 5% of ITT Flygt's turnover. "The key to this case-based approach to development is to use the customer's problems as a design resource. A conventional marketing mind set can be an obstacle to implementing this. Marketing people who think in this conventional way tend to be outward oriented and over-concerned with 'image management'. They see product problems as a threat not a development resource. Of course, when implementing this alternative, 'dirty-hands-on' approach, you still have to keep an eye on the bottom line – we were stubborn about pursuing the farm market because we knew it was potentially very significant. Once you've established that there's significant demand in a new field of application, the task then is to thoroughly understand, ideally from direct personal observation, the business that these customers work in and the problems they confront."

The submersible mixer is able to generate a "jet flow" inside a tank. The mixer can be positioned to direct the flow, ensuring that there are no "dead corners" in the tank. By providing farmers with a package of mixer-plus-pump, the manure handling problem was solved. Having created the submersible mixer, it then became apparent that it had many other applications: Flygt's sales force, with its well developed networks in municipal waste water treatment, immediately began to sell it to sewage plants. Hjalmar comments here that, "if we'd developed the submersible mixer specifically for municipal plants, the sales force would have been opposed to it from the start because it replaced pumps that Flygt was selling to them in several applications."

A fish farmer calls

Hjalmar also began to investigate the mixing processes required in the pulp and paper industry. In addition, fish farmers, quite spontaneously, began buying submersible mixers to generate water exchange in their fish pens. (This is often necessary both to raise the oxygen content inside the pens and to expel waste products from the fish.) "I don't think Flygt as a company knew anything about this until I got an enquiry from Norway; a fish farmer was asking if we had any smaller mixers. At that time the smallest we made was powered by a 14 kW motor. This was really too big for fish farm applications. We established that what they really needed was a 2 kW unit. I told him that if he ordered 30 of them, we'd produce it – which lead to the introduction of our small mixer range." Today the submersible mixer is used for applications in almost the same very broad range of industries as the pump.

Marketing the submersible mixer

Leif Carlsson came to ITT Flygt (from Atlas Copco) as marketing director in 1983. One of his first major tasks was to formulate a marketing strategy for the submersible mixer. Prior to this, Flygt's sales and marketing of this product had been pretty erratic and reactive. "There were a number of barriers to be overcome for product acceptance; firstly, there was still skepticism regarding the use of a submersible motor – though we'd made quite a lot of progress on this issue in connection with the submersible pump. Secondly, submersible mixers require motors which are 30% to 50% smaller than those for an equivalent conventional mixer. Even though this means a corresponding energy saving, potential customers needed a lot of persuading that the smaller motors could actually produce the same mixing effect. As a company the main problem we faced was that, while we were well-known as a pump company, we had no reputation in mixing – we had to build this from scratch."

"We also knew that our competitors would not be far behind us. The technology did not protect us – if you can make a submersible pump, you can make a submersible mixer and we already had a number of strong competitors on the pump side. So, we decided to differentiate ourselves on the basis of how to apply this new technology. Conventional, dry-mounted mixers had been around for a long time and there were a number of well-established 'rules of thumb' about how to use them. Submersible mixing is completely different, so these rules didn't apply and since the product was brand new, nobody really knew how to apply it. So, we decided to find out and turn this knowledge into a competitive edge."

The "high science" route

Lars Frisk, a Flygt engineer who previously ran the company's pump systems department, was appointed to head up a new mixer department. "There were really two ways of tackling this problem," says Frisk, "we could have taken a pragmatic 'trial and error' approach or we could have gone for a 'high science' solution – we chose the latter." Consequently, in the mid-1980s Flygt established a mixer laboratory at its Stockholm headquarters and hired in a scientific specialist in the form of Dr Staffan Rizzler, who had a PhD in sedimentation processes in waste water treatment from Lund University and was (immediately prior to moving to Flygt) an Assistant Professor at the University of Luleå. "Staffan had the sort of knowledge of flow processes that we needed. He more or less developed the concept of 'jet flow mixing' in connection with our submersible product," says Frisk. "The key to applying this knowledge for our purposes was what we call 'sizing' the mixer, i.e. determining the strength of jet thrust, in Newtons, that needed to be generated for a particular application. The variables that affect this include: the capacity of the mixing tank, its shape, and the nature of the liquid being mixed."

Case-specific field trials

Having accumulated a theoretical and experimental knowledge base, Flygt then set up two major field trials; one for waste water treatment applications and one for the pulp and paper industry. "We took waste water first because this was an application where we already had a strong brand as a pump maker." Leif Carlsson points out. The waste water trials were conducted at a treatment plant in the UK. The other trials were held at a small, experimental production line operated by the Swedish Pulp and Paper Institute in Stockholm. "Our motivation in running these trials was to establish databases for submersible mixer sizing parameters in, respectively, waste water treatment and pulp and paper applications. This knowledge put an effective tool into the hands of our sales force."

"In other application areas, such as fish farming, mining, and agriculture, the parameters don't need to be as precise as they do in process industry. Here we learned a lot from our customers," adds Lars Frisk. "Many customers seized on the submersible mixer as a potential solution to a problem they'd been living with for some time and were willing to try it out even without any prior knowledge of how to apply it in their application," notes Leif Carlsson. "Its use in spray painting systems in automotive manufacturing is an example of this." Another, even more exotic, application was the use of the submersible mixer to keep water free from ice in sub-zero temperatures. "Frankly speaking," says Lars Frisk, "some of these applications were more trouble than they were worth, but we didn't know that when we started working on them. The whole market was pretty much 'virgin' territory in those days – you staked a claim to an area and worked it to see if it held anything of value – and, of course, other people could come in and do the same."

"We can say that the submersible mixing really became an established technology in our first target area, waste water treatment, around 1990," says Leif Carlsson. "We can say this with some confidence because it was at about this time that our competitors started seriously trying to move into this market. Pulp and paper is maybe a little bit behind in this development, but is definitely on the way. A distinct problem here is that our sales are mainly based on directly replacing a conventional mixer with a submersible one and process industries are notoriously conservative about making this sort of technological change." Lars Frisk adds that, "at the beginning we thought that in order to succeed in pulp and paper we had to be a 'total mixer supplier'; in other words, that we needed to offer a product for each mixing application in the industry. Now, however, we've realized that it's OK for us just to concentrate on the mixing niches where submersible is the best solution – though, again, this is something we've learnt with experience over the years, and I would say it also applies to other industries. We now have much more of a 'niche applications' strategy – though there are still lots of potential applications that we really haven't addressed at all yet."

Company-wide effect

"In addition to now providing about 5% of our turnover, the submersible mixer has also had a quite profound effect on Flygt as a company," says Leif. "Adopting this 'know-how' strategy to market it meant that we got deeply involved in trying to understand the chemical and biological process of waste water treatment. This lead us to adopt other new products, such as aeration diffusers, and also turned us into much more of a 'systems know-how' company, than a simple product manufacturer. An example is our 'racetrack' package" (see page 182).

Ericsson is planning to become a major player in the next phase of wireless communication: machine to machine. Unlike the mobile phone, this is very much a B2B product area, involving complex value chains with many different B2B actors. Ericsson's marketing strategy in this area is to pedagogically present the possibilities to the various actors, encourage them to form the necessary value chains and to develop long-term supplier relations with the initiative-takers. A key element in this strategy is the use of a case-based approach.

M2M – the next phase of wireless communication

The market for mobile telephones has grown rapidly across much of Europe, North America, and the rest of the industrialized world. Mobile phones, however, are becoming increasingly commodified – the next major growth area in wireless communication will be in the area of machine-to-machine, or man-to-machine (M2M) communication. The key product here will be the wireless communication module: Ericsson is using its expertise in communications infrastructure and radio frequency technology to design and manufacture a range of small devices that enhance the management and profitability of machine-to-machine communications over cellular radio networks. Called wireless communications modules, they are integrated within other equipment and are used in many different telemetry applications for making short message service (SMS) calls or automatically sending data and voice messages to a control center. They are being integrated in automobiles, fleet management systems, fire and security alarms, vending machines, public utility meters, and other electronic office and industrial equipment. Ericsson is also using its knowledge of communications system design and operation to help system integrators, service providers, and network operators to take full advantage of the many benefits and opportunities that these new devices provide. Changes in the software have also been made to allow the seamless transport of data and information. The module will be built into its host appliance, and controlled through a computerized link.

Modules will increasingly be built into a wide variety of equipment, including domestic appliances, industrial machinery, metering equipment, and all kinds of vehicles, and will soon be taken for granted, much as the integration of the microchip is today. Water, electricity, and gas meters are already being read digitally and reported automatically by wireless communication. And we already have houses, or business premises, where a break-in or fire is reported to the authorities without human intervention. And cars which not only call for help automatically after an accident, but which can also identify with pinpoint accuracy where they are, and even give some information about what type of incident has occurred. Modules will thus automate a wide range of existing functions and will stimulate the development of many others, which we cannot yet imagine. This market is potentially significantly larger than the wireless, person-to-person market. The challenge of marketing M2M technology is its more or less unlimited applications – the only boundary is human imagination.

The future

The potential for wireless module communication could be summed up in the concept of: (at least) "one module per house, one module per car." What this means is that, in principle, all communication systems could be channeled through the wireless module – both for the home and the car. A single utility or security company – or the builder – may provide the first module to a household or other premises, and automotive manufacturers may supply a single module to a vehicle for a dedicated purpose. Once this module is in place it can then be used for a variety of different purposes – and customers will come to expect more and more communications system to be channelled through a wireless module. Soon most dwellings will contain several modules: many domestic appliances, such as refrigerators, will be routinely equipped with them. (This is already the case in at least one brand of washing machine.) These "local" modules will report, probably via a LAN network, to a central "gateway" module, which will provide the link between the dwelling and the public wireless network. (Ericsson's Bluetooth, and similar systems are already being developed to achieve this.) The scope for the wireless module is even greater in the B2B world than for these domestic applications: it's generally believed that B2B segments, such as fleet management, remote diagnostics, vending, monitoring of servers, etc., will grow faster and be more significant.

As regards the size of this potential market; a tenfold growth in vehicle numbers is probable worldwide over the next decade, to a total of 500 million vehicles, with an annual increase of 50 million. In addition, in Europe alone there are 100 million households, 10 million vending machines, 4 million alarms and 3 million elevators; each of these has a potential need for wireless communication. On top of this there are all types of metering systems, plus many other types of equipment in which the module has applications.

In conjunction with the development of this technology, we are likely to see the emergence of new multi-service providers; organizations or businesses which don't, as yet, exist: these will act as intermediaries to households in supplying electronic services by wireless communication, including: many forms of entertainment, internet access, telephone services, security systems, and utility services. We can see the beginnings of this in the current spate of mergers between media-entertainment and telecommunications companies and the emergence of "multi-utilities" companies which provide gas, water, and electricity services together. The capital cost savings which wireless modules can offer (in comparison to landline communication) will provide a powerful stimulus for the already emerging integration of these business areas.

An overview of the market for modules

The wireless communication module thus has potential applications in an enormous number of business areas. Anywhere where data can be transmitted from machine to machine, whether this is done today via fixed lines, or whether it could be done in the future, given the technology of wireless transmission. These areas divide into fixed line substitution, and mobile solutions. Fixed line substitution covers telemetry – that is, areas like vending machine monitoring, alarms, metering for utility companies (gas, electricity, water, etc.), parking meters, leased office machines, traffic lights. This category also contains the whole area of service and maintenance, e.g. for lifts and other equipment, and even point-of-sale equipment. Information signals of all types could be controlled by wireless communication. The other area – mobile solutions – would include, for example, personal security equipment and equipment tracking, and everything connected with vehicle communications from entertainment to navigation equipment.

The value chain

The major players, who come together in the value chain, are as follows:

- the supplier/manufacturer of the module (e.g. Ericsson)
- the "system integrator" (e.g. manufacturers of meters or electronic "end-to-end" solutions for vehicles)

- the hardware owner

- the third-party service provider (e.g. a utility or entertainment company)

- the network operator (e.g. Vodafone, Telia)

- the "service operator" (e.g. Maingate, Telia's M2M subsidiary)

- the end user.

Other interested stakeholders, such as finance companies, banks, and insurance companies may also play roles.

The idea behind the role of the service operators is that of an overall initiator and co-ordinator, bringing together the technology and the other actors to create the market. This role could also be played by the network operator or the third-party service provider (there may be a tendency for network operators to also become service operators) but, in principle, any of the five actors could take on this role – including the module manufacturer. These markets are so new that these roles have yet to be well defined. In addition, these value chains will be complex: the allocation of actors to roles may develop differently in different business segments and geographic markets.

An example of this is provided by the main Swedish airtime provider, Telia: it has co-founded a subsidiary called Wireless Maingate specifically to deal with machine-to-machine communication. Wireless Maingate has now also taken on the role of a system integrator, helping to administer the systems of its customers. Maingate is a pioneer in this role, developing closer and closer relationships with customers. In a similar way, many of the companies within the value chain which traditionally may have regarded themselves as simply suppliers, will now have to learn how to nurture close partnerships both with their customers and with the other "module actors."

The wireless module market is an immature one. Its development is still really at the stage of trying to make the cake bigger, rather than competing for market share. In terms of Geoffrey Moore's analyses, from *Inside the Tornado*,[1] the M2M market is still pre-chasm: in other words still dealing with the pioneer phase in terms of product take up. Value chains or value networks have yet to be established. It's still at the stage of team building, of trying to put together networks of players including for example financial institutions. Each of these players must see an advantage in participating.

The benefits of modules to the market

The benefits of module communication to the various actors are summarized below. Arguments to convince network operators, are as follows:

- M2M communication can be programed to use off-peak, relatively unused airtime, increasing operators' load capacity – hence their income – without affecting existing business

- Network operators will also gain large corporate customers – a single customer who will provide a large volume of regular M2M business for them, and it is predictable business which can be planned and managed. These operators will also be entering new and profitable business areas

- M2M communication and subscriptions may also provide network operators with opportunities to bundle the M2M services with other services to the customer, thereby enhancing their total offering.

The benefits for the other actors are threefold:

- Firstly, cost saving and accuracy are almost certainly going to increase where manual monitoring and inspection is replaced by automated wireless communication

- Secondly, considerably more information will be made available through this cheap and effective method of communication. This will allow for system improvements including proactive maintenance – anticipating component and system failure and correcting them before they occur, thus significantly reducing downtime. It will also help in planning and investment decision-making, by providing a detailed and dynamic picture of the relevant customer base and/or geographic region

- Thirdly, module communications may enable organizations to offer additional services, which at present are not feasible or not economically viable.

There are many new business opportunities here. These developments can also be linked to the upcoming move toward mobile internet access. The progress of wireless communication has evolved from people-to-people, to people-to-machine and machine-to-people so the next logical step is machine-to-machine. Along with all the other actors in the value chain, the ultimate consumer will also benefit in many ways – not least (to take a minor example) by always finding the right drink in a vending machine.

The key marketing issues

Two developments are key to unleashing the potential of the module market: firstly, decreases in air-time costs on public networks and, secondly, increases in their bandwidth, to enable a much broader range of communication services to be delivered via the public wireless channel. There are also a number of secondary issues concerning standards, reliability, privacy, and legal requirements.

Price structures

What the price structures will be for the vast majority of potential M2M wireless communication applications has yet to be determined. A number of trends are, however, already clear: the differences in the price structures between network operators and between different countries are slowly drawing closer – and with market volume, this effect is likely to accelerate. A number of costs are almost certainly going to be involved in wireless communication via modules:

- the cost of buying the module
- a one-off installation fee
- a subscription fee
- charges for the communication traffic.

Reliability/signal quality

Several of the potential module applications discussed above, such as video films and computer games, will require greater band width than is currently available via public networks. These hindrances will, however, soon be overcome by new generations of module and wider band width standards which are currently being developed. The increasing use of wireless communication for all types of emergency alarm systems will obviously put greater demands on its reliability as a communications channel, not least from a legal point of view: the US already requires certification of the robustness of public networks and the EU Commission is looking into the issue of wireless communication for emergency alarms, with a view to producing a Directive on the subject. Standards and "roaming" are also important issues in the automotive and fleet management markets.

Privacy/security

The increasing use of wireless communications raises the question of privacy, both for individuals and for companies: for example, making the location of people and vehicles traceable by unauthorized third parties can clearly be regarded as undesirable. Two features of modern communications systems are available to counter these risks: firstly, the growing use of digital rather than analog signals in itself significantly reduces the possibility of third party access, and secondly, if the privacy issue is considered absolutely critical, then encryption is always a possibility. However, information will always be accessible to the authorized personnel who operate these systems. Ultimately they have to be trusted not to disclose this information in illegitimate ways.

Ericsson's role

Ericsson is a world leader in the infrastructure for mobile communication. At present, this infrastructure is used almost exclusively for voice only, i.e. person-to-person communication, but increasingly it will also be used for M2M communication. Ericsson's goal is to also be a key player in this enormous future market, and the company has a number of competitive advantages:

- Ericsson offers a component, the module, and unlike its competitors, Ericsson covers multi-standards (GSM, AMPS, and TDMA) with physical compatibility between different standards. This is especially important for wireless communications modules because their applications may be global

- Ericsson is the world leader in the technology of wireless communication, always in the forefront of technical and commercial developments for mobile communications

- Ericsson, with its long experience and large resources within telecommunications, is able to provide the after sales support which will be necessary when integrating modules into their applications.

TARGET BUSINESS AREAS

The automotive industry market

The potential for wireless communication in vehicles includes such things as –

- entertainment systems
- climate control

- mechanical status reports to dealers or vehicle maintenance centers

- satellite navigation via GPS (global positioning systems)

- traffic information including map guidance and advice on traffic congestion, etc.

There are other possibilities, although further into the future, including immediate accident reporting using the triggering of airbags to signal an alert to the emergency services. The report could also provide an exact location using GPS; seat sensors could provide the number of passengers, and the details of which airbags have been triggered could provide some information about the type of accident, for example whether it was a head-on collision. At present products of this sort are being developed for the high end of the car market, but three to six years down the line they could become standard specification, even in volume cars.

The fleet management/vehicle positioning market

For this application, each vehicle in a fleet will be equipped with a wireless module capable of providing three principal functions – checking the vehicle's position; monitoring and reporting for security, including alarms, etc. and as a backup for, or alternative to, the driver's mobile phone. The module can also be used for vehicle diagnostics.

The utilities market

In this market, modules will be used for remote metering of the consumption of the various utilities, gas, electricity, and water. Other applications in the utilities business area include infrastructure monitoring, involving observation and reporting from water pumping stations, electricity distribution sub-stations, remote switchgear, etc., as well as service and maintenance functions. A typical characteristic of this market is that there may be only one signal every 24 hours from each meter – reporting usage for the period just ended – but at a regular time, which could be during off-peak periods. Customers in this market will be the meter manufacturers, who will buy modules and incorporate them into their meters. The actual service providers (i.e. the gas, water, and electricity companies) will, however, be the main players in the process of introducing modules in the utilities business area. The main business relationship in this market is between meter manufacturers and network operators.

The major market driver in this industry is the increasing introduction of deregulation, as state monopolies are privatized and opened up to competition. The issue of metering becomes very important, with the opportunity to change rapidly between suppliers; for example, in Sweden, consumers may have the option of changing electricity supplier once a month. This market is currently concentrated in Scandinavia (including Finland), North America, and Great Britain, but other markets will follow soon.

The security systems market

This market divides into two: automotive and household and commercial property alarms. The auto alarm sector involves the retrofitting or after-market for alarms, fitted into vehicles after they have been manufactured and sold. The second sector covers building alarms, for households, commercial premises of various types, and other buildings. Security companies are interested in wireless communication for two specific reasons; firstly, because they provide a more secure alarm reporting system, given that physical land lines can be cut or damaged and, secondly, it's a lot less costly to install. And of course, once a household has a wireless communication module in it, many other opportunities are opened up; the module can be used for many other applications. For example, systems for monitoring the wellbeing of elderly people. This is a step towards the concept of the "intelligent house."

Case analysis strategy

The use of business case analyses in promoting the sale of the wireless communications module has several objectives: firstly, it provides detailed information about targeted business areas segments; the goal is to totally understand the customers' business rather than just supply modules as a commodity. In terms of this learning function, a case-based approach is an alternative to conventional, consultancy type market research, involving questionnaires and so on. The case-based approach can provide a much more concrete picture of targeted businesses. This is certainly a second goal – to get to know actual customers by concentrating on actual cases: it can directly generate leads. Finally, it enables presentation packages to be constructed based on cases. The strategy should create a generalized case for each target segment. These should be based on actual visits to prospects and kept constantly updated. For promotional purposes, these cases can be used on the web, sent out via direct mail, placed in the trade press, and salespeople can use them as handouts.

get to know actual customers

by concentrating on

actual cases: it can
directly generate leads

Business case analyses of module applications can be presented to potential customers, such as service providers, network operators, and system integrators. These business cases cover:

- a general market overview
- possible objectives and strategies for the various actors
- a financial analysis of implementing wireless modules for the different parties in the value chain.

These business cases have three objectives:

- to increase the internal understanding of customers' business
- to facilitate a structured strategic discussion with customers and partners
- to use the business cases as an important part of marketing strategy.

Ideal segments which can be developed in terms of this case-based approach are: fleet management and vending machines, and security systems and utilities. The idea is to take a holistic approach to these businesses and aim the presentations at key players. We can take vending machines as an example of the case-based approach.

A business case example: vending machines

In this case "key players" includes: the vending machine manufacturers, the makers of the coin systems for the machines, the owners of the machine (the vending operators), and the owners of the point of sale, which could be a cinema or a supermarket. Installing a wireless module in a vending machine offers a large number of benefits: it enables enormous price flexibility, for example offers on certain items can be made automatically and remotely depending on the local competition for a particular machine. Other payment options can be introduced for example "micro-payments": people could order and pay for goods from a vending machine via their mobile phone. Such payments could, for example, be added to their mobile phone bill. In addition the module can provide an enormous database giving rich and accurate information on the usage of each machine. This data can be used to optimize the positions of machines, the distances between machines and the stock each one contains. Having this data, and these functions, available can potentially increase the pre-tax profits of a vending machine operator by well over 100%.

The strategy is to present specific alternative scenarios where the various actors might play different roles. For example, in the vending machine business we can look at two alternative scenarios for implementing a micro payment system via mobile phones. In the first scenario the key actor would be the vending machine manufacturer: they would provide the initial investment. The manufacturer would need to form a partnership with an application service provider who would manage this specific communication service for vending machines. The manufacturer would then sell or lease the communication platform, i.e. the wireless module and other equipment, to the machine operators. The partners would also need to recruit and co-ordinate the activities of several other players: a telecom operator and access provider to provide and manage the physical communication processes and a content and application provider to support the service, plus an internet payment provider to manage the financial transactions (see Figure 3.3).

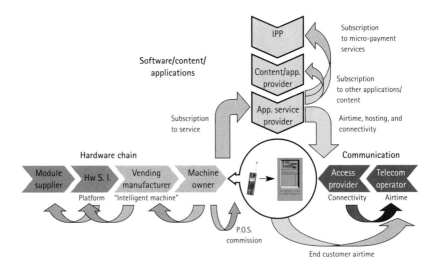

Figure 3.3 Scenario A: Vending manufacturer installs communication platform

A second, alternative scenario would be for a wireless application service provider (WASP) to be the entrepreneur: this is basically the same player who was a junior partner to the vending machine manufacturer in the first scenario, but in this scenario they would need a strong financial partner, such as a bank or a telecom operator. The WASP would take the initiative to set up a particular micro-payment service and would recruit and organize the other necessary players. The WASP would then sell or lease the communication platform to the machine operators (see Figure 3.4). The WASP may simply be a tiny entrepreneurial start-up. On the other hand, the strong partner they're going to need to succeed will be a major national bank or telecom operator, which, ideally, would already be a global player.

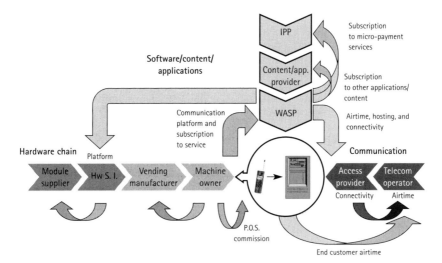

Figure 3.4 Scenario B: Service provider installs communication platform

In the M2M wireless communications business there is no complete product that can be produced and sold by one of the players alone – unless all the necessary players co-operate to deliver these communications services, the product doesn't exist. This is why case analysis is so useful here: it can helped to create the sort of relationships and the sort of co-operation which, as yet, doesn't really exist, but which is going to be necessary to get these businesses launched. The case-based approach is the best way to get people to imagine the possibilities.

MaxMove is a small, Swedish-based company which manufactures and promotes a highly innovative mobile access platform. After a somewhat sporadic start, a new president was brought in to develop and implement a more effective marketing strategy. He's shifting the customer base into aviation and manufacturing, which offer higher value transactions than construction (which was previously the company's predominant segment) and he's using a case-based approach to achieve this.

The product

Mobile access platforms and scissor-lifts have an enormous range of applications: lifting, maintenance, construction, cleaning, etc. A major drawback, however, with conventional platforms is maneuverability: a restricted turning circle makes working in tight spaces difficult – and access through a narrow opening often impossible. The solution would be to devise a means for allowing movement forward, backwards, or sideways – at any angle – and the ability to pivot the machine on its own axis. With conventional axles this can only be done by forcing tires to twist without changing position, which requires considerable power, creates at lot of friction, and causes wear.

Enter the "conical wheel"

MaxMove has come up with two innovations which solve these problems. The first is a conical wheel driven by a vertical axle. This configuration means that each of these wheels – mounted as a diagonally opposed pair on opposite corners of the chassis – can be rolled around its own axis to point in any chosen direction. When drive is applied, the platform can then move in any direction, with the other diagonally opposed pair of wheels, fitted as trailing castors, following the lead of the powered conical wheels. This means that the platform can move forwards, backwards, and sideways in any direction, and even pivot on its own axis. MaxMove's second innovation is a computerized control system which provides the operator with a joystick console and a small lever to select the direction of travel, indicated by an arrow on a clock display. Moving the joystick moves the lift in the direction of the arrow. The further the stick is moved, the faster the speed of travel.

Three-dimensional precision

The result is instant, precisely controllable, maneuverability – in three dimensions if you include the vertical lift ability. This ability to position the platform exactly where it's needed means that the size of the platform and machine can be minimized and its ability to pivot on its own axis makes access through narrow openings quick and simple. This enables the MaxMove platform to operate easily in very tight and confined spaces.

Company history

The "MaxLift," as it was first known, originally appeared on the market during the year 1989–1990. Kramo, the Swedish equipment rental company bought 100 units, which was a big initial boost for the new company. Another boost came from a Japanese order for 60 units in 1995. The real turning point came, however, in 1997, when Axel Wallenberg, from the famous family of Swedish industrialists, bought the company. Prior to this, MaxMove had a total of 15 employees including the workers at the plant in Bjurholm, 60 km north east of Umeå in the far north of Sweden, where the products are manufactured. The company was turning over less than SEK 8 million. Apart from 10% in aviation, all its sales were to the construction industry and 80% of these were to rental companies, who traditionally do not like innovative products. (The inventor of the conical wheel, which is perhaps the key development behind the MaxMove concept, was originally a house builder and so had a definite orientation toward the construction industry.)

Following the change of ownership, MaxMove started its own rental company, "3D-Access." The first rental depot was set up in Umeå, in the autumn of 1998. This depot turned over SEK 1.5 million before the end of that year. The following year depots were established in Stockholm and Göteborg and in Malmö in January of 2000. From 1999, 3D's turnover began to increase, reaching SEK 13 million in 2000 and an estimated SEK 20 million in 2001.

In addition to setting up its own rental business, the new owner also recruited a new CEO, specifically to address MaxMove's strategic marketing problems. The new President was Peter Friedrichsen. Peter's immediate background was three years with the international consultancy firm, BTS, where his speciality was change implementation, but before that his career had been at the truck company, Scania. He'd worked at their main plant, in Södertälje, just south of Stockholm, in both technical and marketing positions. It was mainly this experience in industrial manufacturing that MaxMove was after.

Too narrow a niche

Looking at the company he took over in the fall of 1999, Peter comments that: "its main marketing problem was the narrowness of its customer base – this was a niche of a niche: users of access platforms are a niche within the construction equipment market and even within this group only a proportion of applications need a highly sophisticated platform like MaxMove's. Our rental company could maybe grow a bit more but its demand for new units is decidedly limited."

On top of this restricted growth potential in its main market, MaxMove was also experiencing financial difficulties: "The company's planned turnover for 1999 was SEK 50 million but the actual figure was only SEK 25 million. One of the explanations for this has been an under-estimate of the time lag between our potential customers getting to know about our product and their willingness to actually buy it. For whatever reasons, this period seems to be much longer than people at MaxMove originally thought it would be. The short fall in planned revenue created all sorts of practical problems."

New strategy

It was clear that the company needed a major change of direction. Friedrichsen hired a consultant, Per Hallius, who was an old colleague of his from Scania, and the two of them produced a written plan for MaxMove's future. "The main thrust of our thinking was 'to go where our product will be most valued'. And the key to this value is time-saving: our unique maneuverability saves time in positioning people, tools, and materials. So the next question was, 'where, in which business areas, is this time efficiency most valued?' One obvious answer is aviation – airlines are extremely keen to reduce the 'turnaround' time of their aircraft on the ground between flights. Another major area is manufacturing. I knew, both from my days at Scania and from my work as a consultant, that the real efficiency gains to be achieved in manufacturing are all to do with time-saving. So we shifted MaxMove's target market focus to these two areas."

This strategy had already had effects by the end of 2000: as a proportion of turnover, construction had fallen to 50% while aviation and manufacturing took

25% each. The target for 2001 is 25% from construction and 30–40% each from aviation and manufacturing. "Mindful of previous under-estimates of the duration for new product up-take, we looked at this issue for these two areas and came up with estimates of; three months to one year for aviation and six months to four years for manufacturing."

Reference cases

But, how to break into these new and difficult markets? MaxMove was, in fact, already in the aviation market in a small way: they had sold equipment to the Swedish military, SAS, and Korean Airlines. "These deals came about, I'd say, from serendipitous personal contacts rather than any systematic marketing effort," says Peter. "Our new owner, Axel Wallenberg was trained in aeronautics and there were a number of real lucky chance meetings at exhibitions, etc. This however was a very good start – reference cases like these are a real 'door-opener'. Getting commitment from major players in the aviation business, though, is another matter: it's all based on networking."

MaxMove has an example from one of the world's major aviation manufacturers: "They were interested in our technological presentations and would come back with specific questions, but after a while we got the impression that this could be an end-less process that was never going to lead to a sale. Then, however, we appointed a company with whom they already had a relationship as our agents for the region they're located in: our new agents both sell and maintain forklift trucks and access platforms in their plants. When they found out about this, it was as if we'd suddenly become an 'insider' in their world – then they were ready to do business with us and we got some orders." Partly as a result of this experience, MaxMove is now looking for a major global partner in the aviation business. "This will almost certainly be a supplier of service equipment to the major global players, who are our target cus-tomers. These are major airlines and aviation service contractors. This group consists of less than 100 organizations worldwide."

Case-based sales and promotion

As regards manufacturing, MaxMove's target is the heavy engineering end of the business, though potentially this is still millions of companies worldwide. "Our immediate specific targets in manufacturing are in aviation, trucks and buses, mold and die moving, and specialist vehicles," says Peter. "Our strategy is to provide 'mobility-productivity solutions'. This means that rather than simply offering manufacturers an additional production tool; we intend to be in the business of partnering them in the development of optimal production solutions in which our product will be a central element. If this strategy is to be successful, we must acquire a deep understanding of the particular manufacturing application in each case. Given this, the obvious way to promote it is to publicize those where we have achieved this and then come up with a solution which customers themselves accept as superior to their previous way of doing things."

He cites an example from an existing customer, the train-maker Adtrans, located at Kalmar, on the east coast of central Sweden. "They'd already bought a side-opening platform from us. But our real opportunity came when they completely re-built their plant: a 'grill' floor was installed where previously they'd used an air-cushion device to maneuver heavy doors into position for assembly. Initially, they simply wanted us to quote for a unit capable of carrying these doors. However, they agreed to allow us to come in and analyze the entire assembly process and eventually, by working closely together, we came up with a completely integrated process which took full advantage of our product's sophistication and flexibility: the doors are now sub-assembled directly on the MaxMove unit, which moves them to the carriage and positions them for attachment in a single movement – thus optimizing the whole process."

 ## FROM STRATEGY TO BRAND

Hopefully, these three cases have demonstrated the importance of a sharp case-focus and the mastering decision criteria from particular applications. As suggested in Chapter Two, this mastering of decision criteria can be seen as one half of the B2B marketer's job. The other half being brand building, centered around the projection of competence. It's to this that we turn in Chapter Four, starting with the differences between branding for B2B and B2C and followed by a look at two real-life cases of B2B branding.

NOTES

1. Moore, G. (1998) *Inside the tornado*. New York: John Wiley & Sons Ltd.

chapter four

BRANDING FOR

B2B

This chapter considers:

- the elements that make up the "brand relationship"

- how this differs between B2B and B2C, and

- what case-based marketing can contribute to initiating and maintaining B2B brand loyalty.

The second half of the chapter consists of practitioner accounts of two processes of global B2B brand building, one from ITT Industries and one from Alfa Laval.

Creating brand loyalty is really what marketing is all about. (See Carl Eric Linn.[1]) But what exactly does it mean to say that a customer is loyal to a particular brand? The first point to make here is that brand loyalty, as an effective force in marketing, exists only in the brains of customers. It's concerned with how such individuals make evaluations between alternatives and with how and why customers are willing to enter into a "relationship" with a particular company (rather than merely conducting single trans-

creating brand loyalty

is really what

marketing is all about

actions with it). "Relationship" appears here within quotation marks because, after all, a company is an organization and not a human person. However, the notion of brand as a surrogate personality, involving aspects such as character and reputation is now well established in the discourse on branding. But just what sort of relationship is this bond of brand between customer and company? Is the nature of this bond different in the B2C compared to the B2B world?

A MARRIAGE-BRANDING ANALOGY

Perhaps the best relationship analogy for a company seeking a brand loyalty commitment from a customer is that of a suitor seeking a marriage partner. This branding/marriage analogy depends on the idea that there are strong similarities between the long-term relationships established by companies with their most loyal customers and the institution of marriage. We can identify three such similarities.

Mutual selection

Companies are obviously looking for customers and the more successful of them target particular, well-defined groups with whom the company believes that it can establish long-term, mutually beneficial relationships. Customers too are looking for suppliers – companies which can satisfy their particular needs and wants in an optimal and reliable way. Once they find what they consider to be the best competitive offering, they will want to maintain a long-term relationship with that company.

Trust and identity

Both marriages and branding are ultimately based on trust. Companies trust their customers to abide by explicit and implicit agreements over payment and to remain loyal to them as long as they are providing the best competitive offering. We shall look in some detail below at the complex elements of trust which can keep customers loyal to a company.

Long-term relationships

This entails that the identity of the other partner becomes crucial. In both the "one-night stand" and the "one-off" transaction, mutual anonymity does not hamper a simple and very short-term exchange of basic satisfactions. When the relationship becomes long-term, however, the deep identity of the other – their real qualities and characteristics – will inevitably emerge during the course of the relationship. The reactions of the two parties during this process of gradual revelation (varying from delight to shock) will determine whether the relationship (which both parties initially hoped would be mutually beneficial) can, in fact, be maintained.

Marketing

Marketing, in this analogy, can be cast in the role of trusted confidant to the lovelorn but hopeful company: its task is to advise the company how to win the commitment of the customer-base of its desire (and, once won, how can it keep them faithful). The company's prospects are in one of two conditions: either they are keen to preserve the pre-nuptial promiscuity of a life in the commodity market of classical economics. The only considerations to trouble them here are ensuring that they pay the minimum price for the maximum benefit – irrespective of both who is currently offering this and from whom they last bought it. Alternatively, they may currently be securely locked in the branded embrace of a rival company. Either way, encouraging them to break their current pattern of behavior is going to take a lot of persuading. How can it be done? And is success to be achieved in a different way in the B2B as opposed to the B2C world?

THE ELEMENTS OF "BRAND TRUST"

Let's take the how to question first. To understand how to induce customers to commit to a brand relationship, we must understand something about the nature of the trust on which it is based. What does it really mean to say that a customer trusts the brand of a particular company? This trust can, in my view, be broken down into five distinct beliefs about this company. These are the "elements of brand trust" (see Figure 4.1) and they are:

what does it really mean to say that a customer trusts the brand of a particular company?

- competence

- probity

- continuity

- "caring" and "value resonance."

(This order, more or less, reflects their importance in terms of historical development.)

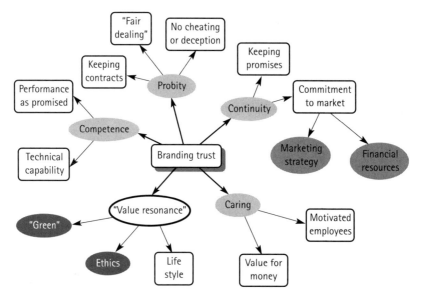

Figure 4.1 The bases of trust – the elements of brand loyalty

Competence

This expresses the basic notion that in order for a prospect to trust a company, he or she has to believe that the company has the technical capability to competently make the product, or effectively deliver the service, they are offering. In other words, the belief that the company has the knowledge and skills necessary for the business it's in – when you buy a radio from an electronics company you expect it to work, i.e. that your new device will be able to deliver the functions consensually defined by the word radio.

Probity

The belief that the company will conduct its transactions with the customer in an honest and fair way, i.e. it will not engage in cheating or deception. This comprises honesty in the legal sense of keeping contracts; that the company has a reputation for "fair dealing," i.e. it is not likely to attempt to cheat or deceive its customers, nor knowingly to subject them to unethical or criminal treatment in any way. (These first two elements, competence and probity, define "trust" in most human relationships.)

Continuity

The belief that the company has the resources and commitment necessary to remain in the business area relevant to the customer, i.e. that it's not going to "disappear" and abandon the customer. This means the belief that they are committed to the markets – both geographic and business – which are important to the customer, i.e. having made implicit promises regarding customer relations, the company is not going to suddenly disappear from a particular marketplace. This is obviously very important in relation to products which have a long lifetime, which may require after-sales support and/or someone to whom complaints can be addressed. Faith in continuity will often implicitly involve two subsidiary beliefs: that the company in question has the financial resources necessary to maintain a long-term presence in relevant markets and that the company's marketing strategy is consistent with this.

Caring

This comprises everything that can be subsumed under the rubric caring – that the company's employees are sufficiently well-motivated to care about the quality of service or performance they deliver, that the company is concerned that its customers get value for money, that the products and services they deliver are of the best possible quality, etc. This element may be a more modern development, in the sense that it rises in prominence in conjunction with greater customer choice, i.e. in situations where there are many market actors who are able to fulfill the basic trust requirements of competence and probity.

Value resonance

This is also a modern phenomenon and has two levels: a basic corporate-good-conduct level and a personalized level of "life-style appropriateness" (which, as we shall see, is mainly an issue for fashion-driven, consumer products). At the basic level, the idea is that customers are more likely to commit and remain loyal to companies with whom they generally share a similar outlook on major social questions. Examples would be issues such as environmental protection and questions of corporate ethics, i.e. child labor, the exploitation of minorities, etc. Over recent decades, a credo of political correctness (which is generally taken to reflect the values of advanced, post-modern societies) has evolved. Large companies, with strong brands (i.e. the ones who have reputations to defend) have become very anxious not to be seen to have violated this credo in any way and will (for very good reasons) go to great lengths to avoid the formation of any such perceptions in the mass media. Where major companies are publicly perceived to have behaved badly in relation to these values, they may well suffer significant economic damage as a consequence. (The situation of Shell in relation to protests from environmental groups over its plans to dispose of its Brent Spar oil platform is a case in point.) This basic level of value resonance applies in both consumer and B2B branding. All types of purchaser may seek to punish the misbehaving company – individuals from motivations of conscience and conviction, other companies (possibly) simply to avoid guilt by association. Consequently, brand loyalty may require the customer's belief that the company in question will not violate the value consensus on environmental and ethical issues.

A company which can inspire high belief scores in all these criteria can be said to have a strong brand and its products will have meta-value (Carl Eric Linn) and can command a premium price. Note, once again, that all these elements can be subsumed under the concept of trust. The point about this is that all trust is ultimately a leap of faith. In addition, the different elements of brand trust may be more or less important for different types of customer – which brings us back to the question of differences between B2C and B2B customers.

B2C-B2B DIFFERENCES

Here we can return to the branding/marriage analogy which can be extended historically in order to draw out the contrast between consumer and B2B branding. Consumer branding is much more like the contemporary notion of marriage, whereas B2B branding resembles the old-fashioned concept of marriage. In advanced, post-industrial societies today, the selection of a marriage partner has become almost entirely a question of individual preference. Parents and other relatives are not expected to exercise a veto right, or even any strong influence in this area – let alone making the decision on behalf of the individual concerned. Generally speaking, therefore, this major life-decision is left to individuals' gut reactions (or to put it more romantically, to the promptings of their hearts). Consequently, it can be made impulsively and, whatever the ultimate outcome, no justification to any third parties is conventionally considered necessary.

Old-fashioned marriage

In the old-fashioned concept of marriage (which can be identified as the one which prevailed in the pre-modern West and still prevails in traditional societies) two factors, in particular, differ from the modern concept. It involves the notion that the selection of a marriage partner ought to be the outcome of a rational decision process (often connected with considerations of social status and property ownership, i.e. objective characteristics which are consensually accepted in the public domain). The relatives – if not actually making the decision themselves – have to be persuaded as to the soundness of the individual's choice.

The analogy here is that the B2B purchaser is very much in the same situation as the old-fashioned marriage prospect: they are supposed to choose rationally and they have relatives to answer to – relatives who are not going to accept selections based on impulsive, individualistic preferences. (This is based on the B2B purchase decision process as described in Chapter One.)

B2B–B2C – DIFFERENT BRAND ELEMENTS

We can now return to the elements of brand trust and try to establish the relative importance of these for B2B vs B2C fashion consumers (see Figure 4.2). The basic idea here is that competence is the predominant element of branding trust for B2B purchasers, whereas for B2C fashion purchasers it is value resonance.

Competence – key for B2B purchasing

That competence should over-ride other branding elements for the B2B buyer has to do with the fact that he or she is usually searching for the solution to a particular, well-defined problem. As we have seen, the purchasing decision will depend on the

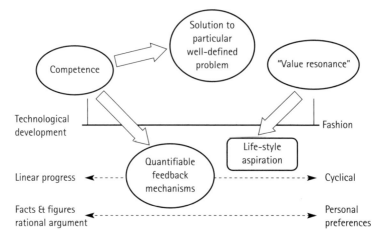

Figure 4.2 Fashion vs Technology: respective dominant branding elements

prospect's faith that the selected company has the competence to solve this problem. Not only this, both parties are also aware that, post-purchase, objective (often quantifiable) processes will test this faith – often coming up with an unequivocal "yes-or-no" answer. If the real-world feedback provides a positive answer, the branding bond between customer and company will be enormously enhanced. Maintaining this bond may well require good performance by the vendor company regarding the other elements of branding trust, but this initial evidence of competence is crucial. Long-term too, in order to maintain the relationship, the vendor is going to have to provide the customer with continuing evidence of competence in the particular technical fields which are important to the customer. (This is also true for individual consumers buying technology products, see Figure 1.2, but B2B purchasers have the added pressure of relatives to worry about.)

Value resonance – predominant for consumer fashion purchasing

In contrast, the most important element of branding trust for fashion-driven, consumer transactions is likely to be value resonance, in the life-style sense (referred to above). As opposed to the corporate-good-conduct level, the life-style level of value resonance is concerned with whether or not the vendor company expresses values which the individual consumer aspires to incorporate into their personal life style. In other words, does this company embody, in the imagery associated with its brand and in all its market communications, a "way of living" (or an approach to life) which this particular consumer might wish to pursue? Clearly, there can be no objective yes or no answer to this question. At the subjective level, some people may react with positive or negative certainty to such propositions – but most people in modern societies seem to be genuinely ambivalent about such questions (and are, consequently, open to persuasion). There's certainly no fashion-driven equivalent to the B2B buyer's objective, post-purchase, competence evaluation. If they are disillusioned, life-style consumers can only really blame themselves for making an error of judgment.

As to locating the other elements of branding trust along the technology-fashion spectrum, they can be distributed (somewhat randomly) between the two extremes. Probity, clearly becomes more important in relation to the size of transactions, and given that transactions in a B2B relationship are likely to have a larger average monetary value than those involved in a consumer relationship, it could be argued that probity belongs on the B2B side. However, consumers occasionally make major purchases too. For similar reasons, long-term continuity (organizations are, after all, potentially immortal) can be said to be more important for B2B buyers. Caring (again, given the proviso of abundant competition) is likely to be relevant to nurturing branding trust in both types of buyer.

THE PROCESS OF B2B BRAND COMMITMENT – A CUSTOMER'S PERSPECTIVE

To return to our old fashioned marriage analogy, we can consider the situation the B2B customer who's in the pre-selection phase of brand commitment. If they're in a small, young company, or concerned with an area of business that for some reason has recently become more important to the company, they may now have become willing to give up pre-nuptial promiscuity and are prepared to enter a committed relationship. Alternatively, they may have become disillusioned with their existing partner to the point where they are willing to contemplate separation and are already searching for an alternative partner. Organizational decision-makers in this situation face three problems:

- how to find eligible partners
- how to judge which of them are most trustworthy (according to the "elements" above)
- having made a selection, how to provide evidence for relatives to support the rationality of this choice.

The immediate answer to point 1 (as Peter Torstensson of Alfa Laval suggests below) is likely to be "front of the mind awareness," i.e. those companies which spring to mind, either privately or in discussion with colleagues and contacts. This poses the question: how have these companies managed to get on this mental short list? An obvious answer here is marketing. In its role as suitor's confidant, marketing, in all its aspects, should have been out promoting its candidates virtues in all the right places. Right is the operative word here, i.e. which channels to use (see Chapter Five for more detail).

The branding power of stories in B2B

Regarding points 2 and 3, what sort of evidence is likely to persuade first the individual decision-maker and then his/her relatives as to the good reputation of a proposed partner? How do you persuade first yourself, and then skeptical third parties, that someone with whom you are proposing to enter into a long-term relationship has a trustworthy character? One obvious solution (which is well-grounded in all human cultures) is to consider the individual's *reputation*, i.e. what do other people say about him/her? This strategy involves seeking out *stories* and anecdotes which people tell about this individual's behavior. As suggested above, in the B2B world the most prised characteristic is technical competence. Consequently, the most effective stories in this context will be concerned with the competence of the proposed partner-company and above all with how they have applied this to the benefit of previous customers, i.e. case stories. Hence the recommendation in this book to adopt a case-based communications strategy (see Chapter Seven). But first we'll consider the experience of two major practitioners in the field of B2B branding.

BRANDING CASE ONE: ITT INDUSTRIES

ITT Industries (International Telephone and Telegraph) is a global multi-industry company which employs approximately 42,000 people in more than 145 countries and has an annual turnover approaching $5 billion. These revenues derive, more or less equally, from its four segments: pumps and complementary products (which is the world's premier pump manufacturer); defence products and services; connectors and switches; and speciality products.

Corporate history

ITT was established in 1920 as an international telecommunications operator and manufacturer. In the 1950s and 1960s it became one of the first classic conglomerates, acquiring everything from bakeries to brake manufacturers, all branded with the "ITT" prefix. Hayes Roth, of Landor Associates comments, "during this period ITT's branding became confused: the name was literally stuck in front of virtually every imaginable product and service. While this contributed to a sense of corporate bulk (the ubiquitous "ITT"), it provided no definition to the brand itself. By the mid-1990s, the whole concept of the conglomerate had generally gone out of fashion and ITT's stock was flat."

In 1995, the ITT empire was split into three entities. One of these was ITT Industries, which became the umbrella organization for several dozen well-known defense, electronics, automotive, and industrial enterprises. To bring some order into the new entity: ITT Industries itself was structured into three management companies: ITT Automotive, ITT Fluid Technology, and ITT Defense and Electronics, each marketing multiple products and brands still bearing the "ITT" prefix. (The current structure was established in 1998 when about 80% of the automotive business was divested and connectors and switches was split off from Defense, as a separate segment.) Though a distinct entity, ITT Industries also had to compete, at this time, for name recognition with the two other new entities: ITT Hartford (Insurance) and the new ITT Corporation (entertainment, hotels, and casinos). The result was that an enormous diversity of ITT "brands" were spread around the world.

Enter Landor

ITT Industries came to Landor seeking a new and comprehensive corporate identity – perhaps even a new name. It needed both to establish itself as a strong brand in its own right in its particular business areas and to distinguish itself from its corporate parent and newly created partners. Landor Associates is one of the world's leading consultancies in the area of brand identity. (Their London office also helped Alfa Laval with their re-branding operation, see Branding case two, page 118). The firm was founded by Walter Landor (1913–1995), who moved from Europe to San Francisco in 1939. "Products are made in the factory, but brands are created in the mind," is one of his keynote quotes, which still drive the organization he founded. Landor applies a four-phase approach to branding:

"products are made in the factory, but brands are created in the mind"

- Audit and analysis – the current situation of the brand is evaluated based on reviews of existing client research, customized brand equity analysis, interviews with management and other key audiences, competitive assessment and site surveys.

- Brand strategy development – conceptual thinking and positioning solutions are evaluated against three criteria:

  - is the brand currently positioned to meet its long-term business objectives?

  - does it own a distinct brand idea that is relevant across the breadth of its business offerings (a "brand driver™")?

  - will this brand strategy endure?

- Creative development – designers work from the identity, branding, and communications strategies identified above. Different design directions are first reviewed by internal specialists and then analyzed in working sessions with the client. The best options are mocked-up and sometimes tested on target audiences before presentation to client management for final approval.

- Implementation – this includes everything from preparing graphic standards manuals to overseeing the installation of signs, fleet livery, website templates, and brochure systems. Introductory seminars and presentations are offered to enhance audience acceptance and periodic internal reviews and field studies are carried out to check consistency and accuracy of implementation.

Landor began working on branding ITT Industries in 1996 and is still (in 2001) working on its brand development. "This has been a major global project for Landor. It represented a significant challenge to us as a branding agency," observes Hayes Roth, Vice President Americas Marketing and Landor's project leader for ITT Industries' branding program. "First, there was the history of a plethora of 'ITT brands.' Second, there was the newly created ITT Industries itself – this consisted of three very distinct management companies headed by three presidents (with real authority) who generally felt their businesses had little in common and that 'branding' was unlikely to solve this problem. All this can be described as a branding specialist's nightmare – or possibly heaven. There was an almost total lack of cohesion and understanding between the component companies and products. The challenge for Landor was to develop a brand for ITT Industries which clearly stood for something. One point of departure was that the company is overwhelmingly B2B – this would clearly make its brand distinct from a consumer company's."

Landor started by carrying out extensive global research. Questions were directed at ITT Industries' customers and employees, the media, and financial analysts. The research indicated that people recognized the "ITT" name and associated it with high quality products. Unfortunately, however, few people associated those products with ITT Industries, mainly because they didn't know which business areas the company operated in. Hayes Roth says, "this was the part of the new ITT that people seemed to know least about. One of the key words which emerged from the research was 'silos'– people saw a lot of separate, unrelated entities, such as defense, automotive, etc. Employees (who are always a key audience) felt that they *really* worked for one of the product-branded business units, such as ITT Flygt or ITT Bell & Gossett. The financial community recognized this was a global company with innovative and high-quality products – but nobody saw a core image; nobody really knew what 'ITT Industries' meant."

Name change?

Hayes Roth recalls that, "a fundamental question which emerged out of all this was: 'should we simply change the name and start again?' Our answer to this was no: firstly, this would be a very expensive solution and, secondly, there was clearly a lot of brand value in the ITT name (though as yet unfocussed). Our strategy instead was to make 'ITT Industries' into a monolithic or 'hero' brand for the whole group. It had to mean the same thing to everybody, despite the fact that the three management companies saw very few links between each other."

Common ground – "mission critical"

Landor's research, however, established that there were links to be built upon: "we identified three broad values associated with the ITT Industries' brand: 'financial stability', 'quality,' and 'reliability'. As reported by the subjects of our opinion surveys, these words overlapped between the three management companies, automotive, defense, and fluid technology, and created common ground between them (see Figure 4.3). Here, on this common ground, we could build our unified brand: ITT Industries produces products which can be counted on to work, even in critical situations. Key words associated with these values were: 'functionality,' 'durability,' and 'mission critical'. This last phrase very much became what we would now call a 'Brand Driver™' in this process; 'mission critical' meant that ITT Industries' products were often employed in situations where, should they fail, human life would be put at risk."

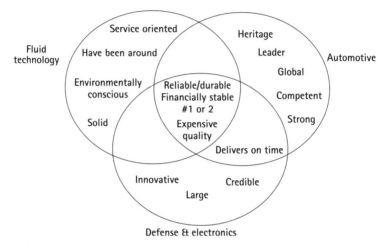

Figure 4.3 ITT Industries' positioning map

The challenge

Tom Martin, senior vice president for corporate relations at ITT Industries, and the man with overall responsibility for the company's branding, comments that, "the issues we needed to address through this branding effort were as follows:

● Brand confusion – our public was not sure of what we did.

● Brand reputation – our reputation didn't match our products, actions, and performance.

● Brand unity – we had multiple product brands and value centers that weren't perceived as part of a greater whole."

On this last point Hayes Roth observes that, "at Landor we recommend a maximum of three 'brand tiers', i.e. vertical levels of identity. When they first came to us ITT Industries had multiple branding levels: ITT Industries the corporation, then the three management companies (ITT Automotive, ITT Defense, and ITT Fluid Technology), then the pre-existing company brands, such as ITT Flygt, ITT Bell & Gossett, ITT Cannon, etc. and even under these there were many specific product brands. It was what we call a very cluttered 'brandscape'" (see Figure 4.4).

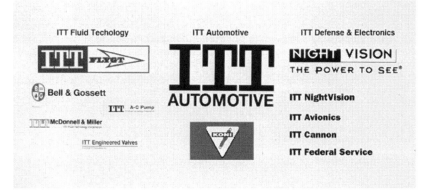

Figure 4.4   ITT Industries' previous "brandscape"

Creating a new logo

Based upon Landor's brand equity research, ITT Industries repositioned itself as a global leader providing highly durable, precision-engineered products. Hayes remembers that, "we tried out many different logo designs and finally (as often happens) returned to one of the first we'd come up with – one that was very engineering oriented." Landor next conducted research on customers' reactions to it: Hayes Roth reports that, "typical responses were: 'big, solid products', 'out of the box' [i.e. innovative and creative] and 'this company builds things [that are] precision engineered'. I'd characterize such responses as extremely positive – this was very much what we wanted."

The new logo (see Figure 4.5) features "engineered blocks," which represent the ITT letters as nine equally proportioned, interlocking elements that come together to form a solid whole. Hayes Roth says, "the new brand mark connotes precision, strength, engineering, and unity. It reinforces attributes common to all ITT Industries' businesses and products. The new design tries to echo ITT Industries fundamental grounding as an enterprise committed to the application of technology to human needs. We also incorporated the new tagline 'Engineered for Life', created by ITT Industries' advertising agency, Doremus, into the signature because we believed it captured the essence of the brand very succinctly."

Figure 4.5   ITT Industries – the new logo

Launch reactions

Tom Martin and the joint ITT Industries-Landor team were convinced that they had the right design concept by February/March 1998. It was approved for launch by the Executive Council of ITT Industries in May 1998. The actual launch took place in September 1998. The PR company, Ketchum, and the advertising agency, Doremus, were commissioned to publicize the launch. "Our principal audiences," says Tom Martin, "were, first, our own employees – and I'd say that it's here that we maybe had the most impact – secondly, our customers, and thirdly Wall Street." Judging by the evidence, the impact on the financial community was also not insignificant: soon after the launch ITT Industries' share value increased by 25% and is now at least higher by a third.

The sub-branding system

On the subject of the company's pre-existing product or "sub-brands," Hayes says "Our strategy was to reduce (or 'rationalize') the extensive number of brands within the management companies unless they could demonstrate strong brand equity. This is something we continually monitor, including the evaluation of 'new' acquired brands. The retained brands are clearly marked as subsidiary to the main corporate or 'hero' brand, with a view to enhancing the strength and cohesion of each. In implementing a sub-brand system like this, it's very important to avoid the impression of an autocratic take-over, however; we spent, and spend, a lot of time with those responsible for the sub-brands ensuring that they too see the mutual advantages in our brand linking system. (A lot of this is achieved via ITT Industries' annual marketing communications meetings, which Tom organizes.) The company has a very comprehensive sub-branding program and, in fact, we're still working on it, especially since ITT Industries, as part of its long-term strategy, is continually acquiring new brands. The sub-branding system helps to integrate these new brands faster and more easily."

Managing the brand

"Our goal is to project both our corporate brand and the already well-established product brands we have within the Group," says Tom Martin. "ITT Industries' corporate brand embodies the values of: global presence, financial clout, management talent, R&D support, and visibility across industry sectors, while the product brands contribute: specific market expertise, distribution channels, brand loyalty, and customer satisfaction. To be seen as representing all this we need to project both a strong corporate brand and strong product brands – it takes both! The corporate brand provides a strong foundation for our product brands: it now dominates trade show displays and is included in our business units' advertising. We also use the new brand in our internal publications and it provides a unifying look to our facilities. Our corporate website design captures our brand personality, as do our business unit sites. Even our business cards project the strength of a unified company."

Using the media

On the subject of projecting the brand via the media, Tom Martin likes to quote Kevin Roberts, CEO of Saatchi and Saatchi, "brands must be more than just a set of attributes with a visual identity. Successful future brands will regard themselves as stories people believe in. The heroes of these stories will be products, services, personalities, even attitudes." When asked what is the theme of ITT Industries' stories and who the heroes are, Martin replies, "the theme is the tagline of our new brand image, 'Engineered for Life' and the heroes are the engineers who produce

successful future brands will regard themselves as stories people believe in our products and services. We want to build on the concepts of 'engineering' and 'life' and add a new concept: the most effective technology is virtually invisible to the user – ITT Industries' products play a vital role in this 'transparent' technology. Beyond merely providing company news, we regularly place case stories and other feature articles in the global trade press, in order to provide a voice for our customers and engineers telling our stories."

"In addition, we've established major platforms for proactive media relations, on issues such as water resource management, the market pricing of water, the shortage of clean, available water and the infrastructure spending needed over next 20 years. We commissioned and published a book *The New Economics of Water*[2] covering these subjects. This contains a very extensive Media Resource Guide and was sent to journalists, opinion leaders, and officials around the world, which helped to position ITT Industries as a major provider in the field. We've also, since 1997, been a global sponsor of the Stockholm Water Symposium & Junior Prize." (The Symposium annually gathers over 600 government officials, industry heads, and NGOs from around the world. The Stockholm Junior Water Prize is presented during the Stockholm Water Symposium.) "Our CEO has delivered a keynote address and other top managers have participated. This provides us with exposure to several key target audiences. All this is supported by our corporate advertising, which was initially designed to break through the pre-existing clutter."

As to the future, Martin says, "We'll continue building our corporate brand and linking it to our product brands. We'll find new opportunities to give meaning to 'Engineered for Life'. We're linking advertising and public relations programs in a co-ordinated communications approach. Underlying this is the conviction that branding within the Group is everyone's job – we're interested in deeds, not words."

BRANDING CASE TWO: ALFA LAVAL

Alfa Laval was bought by the owners of Tetra Pak in 1991. Following this, it adopted a logo based on the design of Tetra Pak's logo. When, in 1999, the Group board of Tetra Laval decided to divest Alfa Laval, it was obvious that the logo would have to be changed. In addition to the change of ownership, there were also some organizational changes. For example, the old agricultural division of Alfa Laval remained within the Tetra Laval Group when the rest of Alfa Laval was bought by the private equity investment company, Industri Kapital. This "new" Alfa Laval has a predominantly industrial focus, with food processing representing 20% of its business and marine equipment another 20%. The logo change, required by the change of ownership, was seen as an opportunity to carry out a major re-branding of the company.

Peter Torstensson, vice president of corporate communications, was recruited into Alfa Laval to oversee the re-branding process. He came to Alfa Laval from a Swedish branding agency called Borstahusen. He'd joined the agency in 1991 and became their managing director in 1992. When the top management group in Alfa Laval initiated the re-branding process, they began working with Borstahusen and, shortly after, offered Peter his current job. Torstensson says that, "branding is *more important* in B2B than in consumer marketing: high quality products are just the entry ticket to the market these days – if you want to stand out and succeed, you have to have a strong brand." He goes on to explain this in terms of the B2B buying process: "It starts with a need – but not for a specific product! Customers will ask themselves 'who can help me with this problem?' They're likely to come up with three to five company names. These names come from their own 'top of mind' awareness and may be also from that of influencers close to them. Getting on that initial shortlist is what branding is all about – and the stronger your brand, the more likely you are to be at the top of it. B2B *products* are becoming increasingly similar. In some cases, the brand is the only distinguishing factor."

More than a new logo

The necessity of a logo change triggered Alfa Laval's re-branding and the design of the new logo has provided a focus for the whole process, but Torstensson emphasizes that, "a logo is not merely a design: it is an important piece of the company's brand strategy. We wanted a 'brand mark', not just a graphic identity. The overall objective is to increase awareness of our company and to differentiate ourselves in the eyes of three key target audiences: customers, employees, and the financial com-

"branding is more important in B2B than in consumer marketing

munity." Having established that a completely new design would be required, the London office of the major international design company, Landor Associates (see page 111) was commissioned to assist in the re-branding process and create the new logo design.

Preliminary research – existing value and differentiation?

The process began with research to determine the value and differentiation that already existed in the Alfa Laval brand and to measure the market's awareness of it. "Initially, the internal perception within Alfa Laval was that, after 120 years of operation, the company and its offerings were very well known around the world," comments Torstensson. Landor's preliminary research, however, revealed a more nuanced picture. Bengt Eriksson, who was project leader for Alfa Laval's re-branding process at Landor, explains, "we commissioned a telephone survey of randomly selected purchasers in eight business areas in five countries. These people were first asked to name companies who could supply the sort of products they needed. Then to compare and contrast the products and services they offer. (Though randomly selected, it turned out that about 40% were in fact Alfa Laval customers.)" Awareness of Alfa Laval was high in western Europe, substantially higher than that of its competitors, on average. The figure for the United States was considerably lower and on the same level as competitors there. "Asia was not involved in this survey, but the company's managing directors in Asia were unanimous in their belief that the figure there would have been lower than the result for the United States," notes Torstensson.

Good products, but little differentiation

Where there was awareness, customers and potential customers perceived Alfa Laval as a leading global company, with premium prices, high-quality products, and a financially stable organization. The company's sales representatives were seen as knowledgeable, and its employees as innovative and competent, with a responsive and professional attitude. "The company was perceived as a 'verbal brand', meaning that while the company's products were relatively well-known, requests to describe the logo were very poorly answered," says Eriksson. There also seemed to be a feeling that Alfa Laval lacked the ability to fully understand customers' needs and the will to adequately cater for them. "The focus was very much on the products the

customers are certainly looking for quality products and competent people

company produced, there was very little perception of Alfa Laval as an *organization*," adds Eriksson. In addition, the company's level of differentiation was not high enough to distinguish it from other brands: when Alfa Laval's image was compared with that of its major global competitors using ten different brand image measurements, the curves looked exactly the same.

Torstensson comments, "The fact that we had a generally positive image but lacked differentiation actually provided a great opportunity for us to increase our competitiveness via our re-branding process. We found there was substantial value connected with our name: the market associated us with quality products, good people, good service, and a premium price – but still offering good value. This was a desirable image to have, since it's very close to the general criteria customers use to select business partners – they are certainly looking for quality products and competent people. There was, however, a gap between our image and what customers want in terms of fully catering for their needs. We are, therefore, focussing on exactly these elements both through a re-organization based on market segment and a reinforced emphasis on parts and service."

The "brand driver"

These findings also guided the formulation of Alfa Laval's new brand driver, "the security of change." This brand driver phrase was never intended for public consumption, but rather as an internal guide for the re-branding process. The new public mission is: "to optimize the performance of our customers' processes, time and time again." Torstensson says, "compared to Alfa Laval's previous mission statements, this is much simpler and it's more customer-oriented. The idea now is to see things through the customer's perspective – from the outside in, instead of inside out. Every customer's need is a challenge to us – this is the promise we have to live up to."

the idea now is to see things through the

customer's perspective –
from the outside in,

instead of inside out

Before creating the new logo Torstensson's team carried out an internal audit to see if there were any elements from the company's previous logo designs which could be built upon. "One element was, of course, the Alfa sign (a variant of Alpha, the first letter of the Greek alphabet). This has been part of our identity since 1963. Searching about 45 minutes on the world wide web, we found 15 other companies that use Alpha in their company name and this was not a surprise. Alpha is a generic word and we can never own it exclusively. Each of these 15 companies is using an Alfa sign as its 'unique' mark. Moreover, these companies were all involved in very different types of business – advertising, printing, insurance, finance, even golf." The conclusion was that the Alfa sign did not have potential for development.

"We had two challenges in coming up with a new design," explains Bengt Eriksson, who led Landor's core team of six people in the design process. "Firstly, Alfa Laval is an old company heading into a future that looks very different from where it came from. It's a challenge to take a step that is big enough to really send a signal that something is happening without alienating employees and Alfa Laval customers. Secondly, from a customer perspective Alfa Laval was a product brand with positive attributes, but customers really didn't see or think about the company behind the product. In the future, however, I think we'll see that the company itself will play a more important role and that there will be a greater component of service and really helping customers to improve their processes. I also believe that the new logo will be a tool in the change process of the company and of how the market will look at Alfa Laval."

The new design

The actual design they came up with uses a standard shaper repeatedly (in different orientations) together with horizontal and curved lines to form the letters of Alfa

Laval's name; the horizontal and curved lines represents global presence (see Figure 4.6). Having been fine-tuned by a team of seven senior Alfa Laval managers, the design was ready for testing. Landor's first test was an internal one: the design was circulated amongst the company's leading communications professionals. (Landor has about 1,000 employees distributed among offices across America and in Mexico, London, Paris, Milan, Madrid, Hong Kong, and Tokyo.) Bengt Eriksson explains that "we asked them to comment on three questions: What sort of characteristics does this design convey? Does it, to your knowledge, have similarities with any existing logos? In your judgement, is there anything in the design which might give cultural offense? The idea of this internal test is to establish that there are no fundamental problems which would block further development of the design." There was also a legal test. Peter Torstensson says "we needed to be sure that we could legally own this design. A survey of 12 countries returned the answer yes."

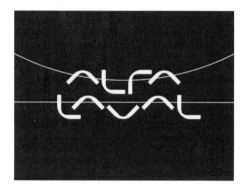

Figure 4.6 The re-branded Alfa Laval logo

Customer reactions

"As regards customers' reactions," says Bengt Eriksson, "we first showed the design to about 30 long-term customers of Alfa Laval in various countries. In one-to-one interviews they were asked how they felt about it: what type of company or business did it seem to symbolize? Was it traditional or futuristic? Product or people oriented? Did they like or dislike it? In general the results were positive, although some criticisms were incorporated into the next phase of developments." Finally, came the market test: a qualitative survey conducted in five countries covering Asia, the Americas, and Europe. Only one person responded negatively to the design. The rest ranged from positive to very positive. "The response to the new design has been very good," says Peter Torstensson. "People say the brand mark reflects a company on the move, a company that is future-oriented, looking more toward what is coming than into the past. Many said it stimulated them intellectually as well as visually, some people see the identity as Scandinavian, while others see it as American or Japanese. I'm happy about that because it means the design is very international."

"Many customers seemed completely stunned by the new logo," says Bengt Eriksson, "they hardly recognized Alfa Laval. The surprise, however, was overwhelmingly positive: they said it evoked a company that was changing – which is good because it highlights the *organizational* image, while the 'Alfa Laval' name preserves the 'old value' of high quality products. They also said it looks smart, intelligent and conveys a sense of speedy reactions." Here are some actual quotes from this research:

> Swedish customer: 'This is a brave thing to do. It really challenges my image of the company. But I think I like it.'

> Japanese customer: 'The design does not suggest hardware. It looks more like software, something intellectual.'

> American customer: 'The lines look like the earth and the sun.'

One clear direction

As part of the re-branding process a booklet "One clear direction," was produced for employees. This describes the company's vision and its new basic core values; "think fresh, be courageous, work together, and act now." "These core values are designed to guide employees when making decisions and conducting business," says Peter, "one of our major ambitions with the design was to try to incorporate these core values in the new logo." As part of the one direction policy, some 20 different in-house magazines, which were previously produced by various centers within the Alfa Laval Group, have now been closed down and consolidated into one customer magazine and one employee magazine for the whole Group. "A major theme of the 'one direction' approach is to mark that the company is now more concerned with 'softer' things, such as building new relationships, rather than simply selling products," Torstensson concludes.

B2B BRANDING – MORE DIFFICULT, BUT WORTH IT

Based on this and other branding process experiences Bengt Eriksson summarizes that, "building a brand is generally a more complicated task for a B2B than a B2C company: in B2C there's a fairly simple product-brand connection, which impacts mainly on customers. Whereas for B2B the link between brand and organization is closer and more important. So, in addition to customers, the quality of the brand can have more impact on the behavior of all those who are concerned with the organization as a whole, e.g. employees, investors, suppliers, political communities, etc. The risks in B2B transactions are generally bigger and more serious, so the generation of trust is one of the major tasks in B2B branding. And this is becoming more and more the case, given the rise in outsourcing, partnerships, use of consultancy services, and increases in environmental liabilities." Despite the difficulties and complexities, however, Eriksson concludes that there are major pay-offs: "I'd say that having a strong brand can provide at least three significant advantages for a B2B company:

- it will encourage customers to 'try you out'
- by generating positive pre-conceptions, it can generate a preference for your company
- it can help a company to sustain a premium price policy."

NOTES

1. Linn, C. E. (1996) *Market dynamics.* Stockholm: Meta Management AB, p. 29.
2. Reilly, W. K. (1998) *The New Economics of Water.* New York: ITT Industries.

chapter five

MANAGING THE COMMUNICATIONS CHANNELS

This chapter applies the B2B, "case-based" paradigm to marketing communications ("marcoms") and to managing the various channels which are now available. We shall first look at a model of how companies in general should be advised to go about the formulation of a marcoms strategy and objectives. Then we'll consider how B2B and B2C marcoms differ in contents and methods. Finally we'll examine channel management and selection.

Communicating the vision

Successful companies are driven by a hierarchy of strategic marketing mechanisms. These may be explicitly articulated or simply implicit in the history and culture of the company. At the top of this hierarchy is a non-verbalized vision of what the company is all about. A mission statement, if they've got one, will attempt to capture this vision in words. From this, business, marketing, and marketing communications strategies can be deduced, in this order. The successful implementation of these strategies requires adherence to two principles: integration and consistency. Integration on the intra-organizational level requires that all the mem-

the successful implementation of these strategies requires adherence to two principles: integration and consistency

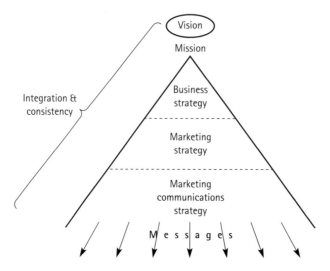

Figure 5.1   A hierarchy of strategic marketing concepts

bers of the organization know and understand these strategies and that they are pulling in the right direction. Extra-organizationally, it's necessary to ensure consistency of the strategies with each other and with the messages which the company projects to its marketplaces. Consistency requires that everything fits together – that there are no contradictions between any elements of the strategies and messages. Both these principles also imply that there should be something of the vision which drives the company in all messages that it projects. (See Figure 5.1.)

Marketing communications objectives

This strategic approach will result in a set of marketing communications objectives. At a basic level, these will consist of: target segments, i.e. identifying your potential customers and knowing who they are. For B2C this needs to be done in terms of demographics, life-style profiles, etc., for B2B it's a question of business areas and professional roles. The next objective is to create "mind share" and, ideally "front of mind awareness" among these people for your company and it's products. In

you need to be **very clear** about
how you **want to be seen**

other words, make sure that they know who you are and what you stand for. Achieving this requires a clear, well-defined organizational identity – *you need to be very clear about how you want to be seen.*

The elements of an identity for a business organization can be divided into three groups. Firstly, the strategy that the organization is pursuing. Examples of the alternatives here can be taken from Michael Porter,[1] is your organization a cost leader, or does it have differentiated products with unique features or is it focussed exclusively on the needs of a well-defined group of customers which it attempts to own? Secondly, what can be called the organization's priority characteristic. (These also relate to its market positioning.) For example, is innovation the main driving force in your company or is quality, or service more important? Thirdly, what values does your company stand for? (e.g. "green," internationalist, etc.) and in what order? It's this particular gestalt of organizational identity, formed from these elements, which ultimately triggers the right-side leap of faith necessary for brand commitment.

B2B–B2C DIFFERENCES IN MARKETING COMMUNICATION

Having considered, in previous chapters, how the B2B and B2C marketing paradigms differ from each other, we can now look at the communication implications ("marcoms"). These can be divided into content and methods (see Figure 5.2).

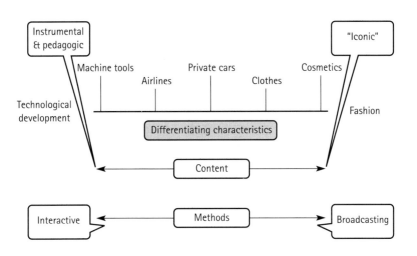

Figure 5.2 Fashion vs technology – communicational differences

To start with content, for fashion-driven, consumer products this can be characterized as iconic, i.e. the content is likely to consist largely of imagery aimed at eliciting emotional responses. For technology-driven, B2B products, however, effective marcoms content can be described as instrumental and pedagogic, meaning that it's designed to communicate information targeted at people who are looking for a product to fulfill a specific, often well-defined need. The pedagogic element will need to be particularly prominent where new technology is involved with which prospects may be completely unfamiliar.

"Iconic broadcasting"

Turning to methods, the ideal for fashion products is "broadcasting." I'm using the term here, not simply to refer to particular technological means of communication (i.e. radio and TV), but rather to express a philosophy of communication. Broadcasting, in this sense, means addressing a mass audience with messages designed for isolated individuals. The messages are likely to elicit direct emotional responses, i.e. people are going to respond favorably to them (and therefore to the product) or they're not. (Whatever social mediation may be involved in this process will be informal and haphazard, via networks of friends and relatives.) The consumer's ultimate decision is individualistic.

For technology-driven products, however, the initial telecommunication (i.e. the original messages delivered from a distance) are more likely (where successful) to initiate a formal group process within the targeted organization, and the message itself will be instrumental and/or pedagogic in nature – directly referring to benefits (ideally quantifiable), which the product has to offer. B2C-fashion-marketers may reasonably expect that some prospects will be likely to buy the product simply from receiving the iconic broadcasting which promotes it. B2B-technology-marketers know that a direct purchase from telecommunications is a highly unlikely outcome: the point of the telecommunications is to get the marketer's product included in the prospect's list of options for evaluation. This will almost certainly require, firstly, at least some discussion between individuals within the prospect organization and, secondly, personal contact between them and the sales organization.

The iceberg of B2B marcoms

Another way to consider this technology-driven, B2B process is via the metaphor of an iceberg (see Figure 5.3). The idea here is that the "random receiver," i.e. the individual

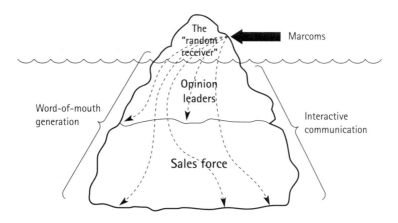

Figure 5.3 The B2B iceberg: the marcom route

within a prospect organization who happens to directly receive the message (probably via an advertisement or editorial item in a trade journal, or by direct mail) is just the tip of the iceberg in a B2B transaction. Their initial interest is just the beginning of the process. If the random receiver is not himself or herself an opinion leader, i.e. a recognized expert in the area of technology in question, they may turn to consultants, technical specialists, or more experienced managers within their own organization or within their personal business network for advice. Even if the random receiver is an opinion leader, they will almost certainly consult with colleagues about the product in which they are interested.

This can be described as the first sub-surface layer of the iceberg and is all about generating word-of-mouth awareness of the product and stimulating interactive communication with the sales organization. Under this is a second, potentially thicker layer, which consists of the sales force "recycling" messages broadcast by their organizations during their personal contacts with customers, prospects, and general business contacts. (As I shall argue later, this works best with published feature articles, but could also be done with published press releases – and, in fact, brochures often involve a recycling of published advertisements.) By handing out material like this during personal meetings, salespeople themselves can try to stimulate this word-of-mouth, interactive communication process.

The pyramid of consumer marcoms

The marcoms metaphor for fashion-driven, consumer products would be a pyramid (see Figure 5.4). Here the random receiver is by far the predominant layer: consumer marketing communications activity is aimed at getting the random receiver to buy the product directly and, as explained above, advertising is the most appropriate channel for achieving this. There is, of course, a role for opinion leaders in this process, though interestingly there's often an attempt to incorporate this function into the advertising itself in the form of celebrity endorsements. (There may also be a complex network of word-of-mouth communications, involving opinion leaders at the local community level, but again, in contrast to B2B, this is unlikely to involve direct dialogue with the company in question.) The sales force may also have a role: customers may want to talk to staff in department stores, and so on, about, for example, cosmetics. The basic idea here, however, is that personal selling is much less important in influencing decision-making in fashion-driven, consumer sales than it is in B2B purchasing.

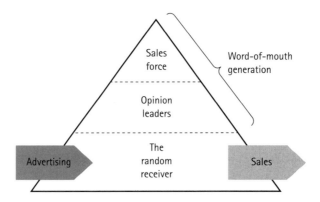

Figure 5.4 The pyramid: simple consumer marcoms

CUSTOMERS' SOURCES OF INFORMATION – MARCOMS CHANNELS

A marcoms channel can be defined as any distinctive means by which customers and suppliers can communicate and transact business. The main sources of information about B2B suppliers can be listed as follows: firstly, those based on personal relationships:

A marcoms channel can be defined as any distinctive means by which customers and suppliers can communicate and transact business

- previous direct experience of the company and its products
- word-of-mouth recommendations from relevant colleagues and contacts
- contacts from the company's directly employed sales force
- distributors, dealers, agents, etc.

Secondly, media sources, which can be subdivided as follows:

- the internet
- the trade press
- "not-specifically-for-business," e.g. radio, tv, national daily press, local press, Sunday press, news periodicals, etc.
- financial press.

Previous direct experience

Previous direct experience of the company and its products – assuming, of course, that this has been positive – is certainly the firmest basis on which to build a relationship of trust with a customer. From the supplier company's point of view, however, this basis has several drawbacks. Firstly, by definition it can only have a positive influence on those who are already the company's customers, so if your objective is to increase your customer base additional channels of influence will have to be invoked. Secondly, in today's competitive business environment, the idea that a customer having once committed to company will then remain loyal for life can no longer be assumed.

The marriage analogy is again relevant here: getting married is not the end of one's problems – boredom and disillusionment can set in and there's always the risk of adultery and divorce! Brand loyalty, therefore, like a good marriage requires continual maintenance. The first requirement is for the supplier company to continue to competently perform the function assigned them by the customer company, and, ideally to exceed their expectations. In addition, two forms of relationship need to be well managed – all the personal interactions which the customer has with the company – everything from visits by service personnel to telephone conversations with the company's receptionist. The second type of relationship can be called the media relationship (see Chapter Six).

Word-of-mouth

After direct experience, the next strongest influence is word-of-mouth. Unlike the friends and relatives of B2C, word-of-mouth for B2B buyers generally means recommendations from colleagues and business contacts. The word-of-mouth advice which is acted on, however, does not come from just anybody within this group: it's most likely to come from people who have high status within the relevant industry and/or organization, e.g. top managers, consultants, technical experts, etc. In other words, people whose judgement is trusted and who can be described as opinion leaders within their particular field. The most effective B2B marcoms will influence them and they will, in turn, influence others.

Salespeople

Salespeople can have a powerful influence over purchase decisions and brand commitment, again, because their effect is based on a personal relationship. It's a very expensive method of making and maintaining contacts with customers and prospects. Given that technological developments have recently created many new marketing and sales channels, it's now possible to save high-cost, personal sales visits for just those steps in the selling cycle which really needed it. An example would be the selling of innovative products.

Sales/marketing distinction crumbling

Traditionally, the purpose of the sales force has been to communicate value, while the purpose of marketing was to create value. Now this division is less clear and salespeople must also create value by providing benefits at a reasonable trade-off to costs.

Value here can equate to problem solving, for example, changing direction, i.e. providing an innovative solution which causes the company to move in a completely new direction. With the spread and development of customer data capture the distinction between marketing and sales is breaking down both for B2B and B2C.

The internet

The internet has rapidly become one of the most powerful forces in B2B business: 78% of the business done on the web today in the USA is B2B and Goldman Sachs Investment Research estimate that the value of transactions conducted online between companies will reach $1.5 trillion in the USA by 2004.[2] (By way of comparison, Forrester Research has estimated that total B2C online commerce in the USA will, by 2003, be only $108 billion.) Much of this will pass through B2B Exchanges, which Arthur Sculley and William Woods (in their book of the same name) define as online market which bring "multiple buyers and sellers together (in a 'virtual' sense) in one central market space and enables them to buy and sell from each other at a dynamic price."[3]

In other words, B2B exchanges will lead to a greater degree of commodification in certain parts of the B2B market, e.g. where customers know exactly what they want. This relates to some of Rackham's latest work, where he envisages three types of buyers:

- "intrinsic value" buyers – who know exactly what they want, i.e. they perceive the product in question as a commodity. They are likely to use B2B exchanges to find the lowest price for what they perceive as equivalent alternative offers

- "extrinsic value" customers – they are faced with a problem they don't know how to solve and consequently need consultative help from vendors

- "strategic" customers – they are interested in creating and maintaining long-term relationships with supplier companies.

The internet has rapidly become one of the most powerful forces in

B2B business

Given these kinds of developments, companies are going to have to change the way they manage channels. Traditionally, companies have asked themselves "what is the best mix of channels for our products and markets?" The goal was to use the fewest channels while obtaining the maximum coverage. The idea of trying to use them all was generally perceived as unattractive because of the expense involved and because it was believed it would cause confusion both to customers and within the organization. Another big objection was the conflicts which the simultaneous use of (in effect) "competing" channels might give rise to, e.g. between the sales force and dealerships or between e-commerce and distributors.

Traditional channel management

Traditionally, prospects and customers have been allocated to particular channels according to the following criteria:

- size of the business involved
- customer's geographic location
- the area of business which the customer operates in
- the products which are being sold
- the "first bite" principle, i.e. whichever channel made first contact with the customer.

The general rules of conventional wisdom were: to keep channels apart in order to reduce conflicts, to use a minimum number of channels and (applying rules above) allocate customers to "appropriate" channels.

The new channel realities

But the old rules of channel management no longer work because customers today refused to be allocated to a single particular channel – technology has now made it very easy for them to switch. These new realities require companies to offer customers lots of channel choice. The "average" customer who uses only one channel is also disappearing consequently, it's now a competitive edge to have more channels available to your customers. Now, it's not only what you sell but also how you sell it. The rules of this new reality can be summarized as follows:

Now,

it's not only what you sell
but also how you sell it

- provide lots of channels

- enable easy movement between them

- let customers choose the channels they want to use themselves

- the web (in this context) is just another channel

- enable customers to do more things for themselves within the channels

- integrate as many channels as possible with each other (for example, Schwab has tried to integrate all its various channels such as branches, advisers, website, etc.)

- managing channels is now part of customer relationship management.

All this encourages new ways of using channels in combination, for example:

- "channel hand-off" – e.g. suspects could be first contacted by a tele-sales team, then, as interested prospects, they can be handed on either to the sales force for personal visits or referred to a website where they can select and purchase products themselves

- "channel-splicing" – simultaneously employing two channels, e.g. asking the potential customer to view a website during a tele-sales call or a personal sales visit

- "webalogs" – putting the old channel of a printed catalogue onto your website so that customers can select and purchase products direct from the site.

Much of this new approach of customer-channel-selection relies on a polarization of customer attitudes to the transaction. Rackham calls this "the eroding middle": the idea is that such attitudes can be located along a spectrum which has transactional business, where customers know exactly what sort of product they want, at one end and consultative business, where customers need advice about the solution they are seeking and want an interactive relationship with the supplier, at the other.

According to Rackham, up until about 1998, most customers were in the middle of this spectrum. Now, however, this middle group is disappearing – making channel choice for customers easier.

THE MEDIA SPECTRUM

Turning now to other media channels, the more traditional media can be located along a spectrum according to the media-consumer's motive (see Figure 5.5). (We'll consider the internet as a media channel separately below.) Analyzing these would certainly seem to suggest that for B2B companies, the trade press is the most effective of the conventional media channels: reading the trade press is generally regarded as a task which is done at work. Many of the readers of the trade press are in "professional buying mode." They will be either professional buyers for their organization or people at work who are now, or will be, looking for information on which to base an industrial purchase. Returning to our marriage analogy, this means that the trade press is a potential "marriage market" for B2B brand loyalty – it's the place the unattached turn to in order to find the sort of partners they would like to have.

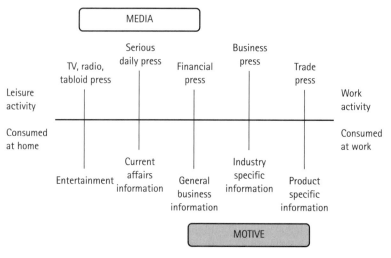

Figure 5.5 The media spectrum

the trade press is a potential
"marriage market" for
B2B brand loyalty

Word-of-mouth for B2B buyers can be strongly influenced by the trade press. As we saw above, this emanates from people who have high status within the relevant industry and/or organization, e.g. top managers, consultants, technical experts, etc. who are likely to be the heaviest consumers of the trade press within their particular business area. Consequently, if your objective is to influence them, then trade press editorial is the channel to use. In addition, opinion leaders may well use trade press editorial to influence others, by for example circulating copies of articles which have interested them.

The trade press has two other features which support this "relationship exchange" role: firstly, in contrast to most other media, the trade press operates on the basis of a tripartite mutual interest. It's the job of editors to publish information about relevant companies and their products, companies want to have this information published and readers have a need to know about it. This information is generally good news (hence the mutual interest), e.g. technological advances and new projects. The second support for the trade press as the marriage market for brand loyalty is the whole apparatus of reader enquiry management, which most trade journals operate. This enables interested potential partners to make contact easily and effectively through the medium of the trade press. (See Figure 5.6.)

SPLICING CHANNELS: THE SALES FORCE AND THE TRADE PRESS

Getting material, particularly feature articles, published in the trade press can also help to overcome the problem of perceived objectivity encountered by salespeople: this is simply the notion that customers and prospects tend to treat what salespeople say about their own company and products with skepticism. To overcome this, salespeople can use trade press material – an example of channel splicing: a

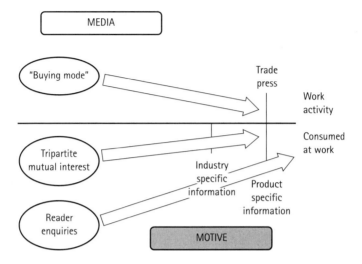

Figure 5.6 The media spectrum – why the trade press?

salesperson can give a prospect a copy of a published article dealing with the particular product that the salesperson is trying to sell to him or her. Ideally the article should be a case story based on a similar application to that of the potential customer and should contain direct quotations from the customer in the case story explaining how the product has solved problems from which he suffered previously. In this way customers from reported cases can make word-of-mouth recommendations globally.

Looking for a moment at the more glamorous end of the media spectrum, i.e. what we called above the not-specifically-for-business media (e.g. radio, tv, daily press, etc.) we can note several points of contrast with the trade press. We can assume that the same individual who reads relevant trade journals at work, will also be consuming not-specifically-for-business media at home. However, the motivations are likely to be different: at work this individual may be specifically searching for a solution and/or a reliable business partner. At home this motivation will be absent, or at least latent. If business interest is triggered at all, it's likely to be in the form of an alert that a particular company should be avoided. This stems from the fact that the majority of editorial coverage in these media consists of bad news. Consequently, companies generally end up in them because they've made a mistake, are involved in a scandal, or have some other sort of major problem.

The financial press can be an exception here – but only if the company in question has good figures to report and even in this case this is likely to influence the behavior of investors rather than customers. Certainly good financial performance may have some positive influence on brand loyalty (the negative is almost certainly true) but this functions only as a passive qualification rather than anything that will lead a customer to commit to a company.

The internet as a media channel

Finally on the subject of media channels we need to consider the internet (as opposed to the internet as a *sales* channel, which will be considered later in Chapter Eight). Since we're recommending that B2B companies concentrate on the trade press, the best approach here is to look at the current situation in terms of the "trade press presence" on the web. This can be summarized in three categories:

- established print journals – most of these now have at least simple websites which promote their journal, as other companies promote their products

- some of these "print-journal" sites include a version of their current print edition, usually in a very "cut-down" form, with summaries of the feature articles, etc.

- a newer phenomenon is the appearance of "pure-web" journals which are published only on the web and have no print equivalent. These are still fairly rare, though growing rapidly as a category.

In terms of influencing mass readerships, therefore, the current position of the internet could be summed up in the phrase "great potential – but not quite yet." There are several explanations for this. Universal participation, even for B2B customers, is still not total, both in the sense of physical connection but also regarding patterns of habitual usage. Maybe more important is the issue of reading convenience; currently available technologies which provide access to the internet do not provide the same level of convenience as print media; for example, ease of reading on planes, trains, and buses. (Though, this, it seems clear, is only a matter of time.)

On the other hand, editors are now browsing the net in search of editorial material and these are the people (rather than the readers of the trade press) for whom it is already an effective channel. A website can be used to promote articles available

"great potential – **but** not quite yet"

for publication to editors and the full texts of articles can be down-loaded or e-mailed to them and then transferred directly into their publishing programs.

 ADS OR EDITORIAL?

Having established that the trade press is the place in which to initiate and maintain B2B brand loyalty commitments, the next question is what is the right balance, in terms of the company's marketing communications resources, between advertisements and editorial? If we consider the process of B2B brand building in terms of the bicameral theory of the brain, the different roles of the two channels can be assigned as follows: advertisements awaken interest in the brand (generally through a specific product offering) via the right side of the brain, which is something which advertisements do very well. For B2B, as opposed to most consumer brands, however, the next step is to deliver complex, objective messages to the left side of the brain, for which trade press editorial is the ideal channel.

If the cost-effectiveness of advertisements and editorial are compared in terms of cost and credibility, editorial comes out the clear winner. It's generally much cheaper to produce and it is usually placed in publications at no cost whatever (an exception being "advertorial" which is normally identified as paid-for space). Advertorial, therefore, suffers from the same drawback as all advertising; low credibility. As intensified competition leads to an ever-greater volume of advertising and, at the same time, readers become better educated and more sophisticated, this skepticism regarding the informational content of advertisements is likely to increase. In addition, advertisements are unlikely to be used to legitimize purchasing decisions, while editorial may be.

"Soap opera" vs documentary

Advertisements can be described as the "soap opera" mode of message delivery because they are subject to few reality constraints. There are policemen (in the form of statutory and other forms of regulation) who endeavor to ensure that advertisements are honest, decent, and legal but there are no third party gatekeepers who decide whether a particular advertisement will or will not be published. In the case of editorial, the "reality-constrained, documentary" mode of message delivery, this role is performed by trade press editors, who have the reputations of their journals to consider.

The organizational advantage

Using the editorial channel to deliver your marketing messages has, in addition, an organizational advantage: conventionally, planning and monitoring the production and placement of advertisements is left to top managers. The company's workforce as a whole usually has very little involvement in this area. With editorial production it's the opposite – people up and down the company have to be involved in: providing detailed information, finding relevant stories, managing editorial contacts with customers, arranging for approvals and illustrations, etc. An editorial activity is reality-based, it ensures that those involved "walk the talk." In other words, producing editorial can serve as one of the mechanisms which can help companies to close the gap between how they would like to be and how they really are (see Figure 5.7).

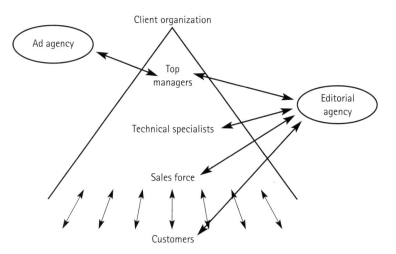

Figure 5.7 Editorial's organizational dimension

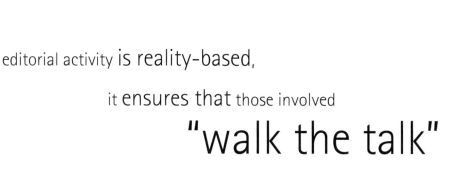

Editorial for B2B brand loyalty maintenance

These and other advantages make editorial the optimal channel via which companies can seek to maintain the brand loyalty of their customers. Its advantages in this regard can be summarized as follows:

- density of frequency (cf. sales visits) – Via published editorial a company can maintain a much higher frequency of contacts with its customers and prospects than it can hope to achieve via sales visits

- cost-effectiveness (cf. sales visits and advertising) – Editorial, can achieve this more effectively and at a lower cost than either advertising or sales visits

- Ease of management (cf. sales visits) – What happens during a sales visit depends very much on the personal relationship between customer and salesperson. Editorial on the other hand, is pre-approved and, once published, is in the public domain

- Reportage vs slogans (cf. advertising) – "Actions weigh heavier than words" – customers and prospects are far more likely to be influenced by the actions of companies (as reported in editorial) than by the simple assertions of advertising copy.

A management challenge – shift paradigms

Given these advantages, why do most B2B companies expend vastly more of their resources (in terms of both money and top management time) on conventional, image-based advertising campaigns than on editorial activity? Let me suggest that the problem here is one of *perception*: as suggested in Chapters One and Two, many people are managing B2B marketing via a B2C paradigm. Consequently, they simply fail to see this opportunity. Without the benefit of the B2B paradigm, advertising looks like the easy option: though expensive and (for B2B companies) inadequate, advertising is relatively easy (from a managerial point of view) to produce. In contrast, the production of editorial (and other case-based promotional material) while more cost-effective, requires much greater organizational co-ordination and effort (though this does have organizational benefits, see Figure 5.7). The argument here is that (as in so many other areas of business activity) overcoming this form of "organizational slack" will provide a competitive advantage in the face of intensifying competition – and the first step is to adopt the B2B paradigm.

☀ SUMMARIZING: WHY PRIORITIZE THE EDITORIAL CHANNEL?

A major point here is that editorial can play a role not simply in the media aspects of sales and marketing but also as a component in the personal-relationship-based forms of selling: opinion leaders may use published editorial material as one of their means of generating and communicating word-of-mouth references and sales-people can use it to overcome the skepticism with which their own statements are often met.

In addition to this, editorial can, in its purely "media" role:

- maintain a cost-effective and interval-dense relationship with existing customers, with a view to maintaining their brand loyalty

- influence decision criteria: i.e. if prospects are in the recognition of needs phase and have not as yet determined the decision criteria by which they will make their purchasing decision (see page 30) then reading about similar customers who've already been through this process can have an influence (favorable to your product) on the way in which they formulate their decision criteria

- provide B2B purchasers with material evidence to justify their purchasing decisions and brand loyalty choices within their organizations.

Chapter Six gives some practical advice about how to produce and place editorial material, then Chapter Seven considers some real-life examples of case stories and technology presentation articles and how they can be used to strategically influence opinion formation in B2B markets.

NOTES

1. Porter, M. E. (1993) *Competitive strategy*. London: Free Press.
2. Scully, A. B. and Woods, W. A. (1999) *B2B Exchanges*. Hamilton, Bermuda: ISI Publications.
3. Ibid, p. 7.

MAXIMIZING

THE EDITORIAL

CHANNEL

An effective practitioner within the B2B paradigm will have a case-based focus. In terms of B2B marketing communications, this means giving priority to the production and placement of *case stories* in the appropriate trade press. This is the natural home of the case story: the trade press of a particular industry or business area can be compared to its nervous system – it's the locus in which information about what's happening is gathered and exchanged. To invoke our legal analogy again, it also has many of the characteristics of the court room – trust and reputation based on adherence to the rules of evidence, and for B2B marketers it's the ideal public arena in which to engage in rational discourse about their products and services. In this chapter, therefore, we'll look at how B2B marketers can maximize both the placement and impact of their editorial material in the trade press.

A clear voice in the editorial lecture hall

Step one is to ensure that your organizational identity is clear, well-defined and completely appropriate for your company and its markets: trade press editors like clear messages. The editorial pages of the trade press, relevant for your business area(s), can be compared with a lecture hall (or seminar room) in which your company may be invited to deliver its messages, as can all the other major actors involved in your markets. Trade press editors can be compared to both debate chairpersons and potential critics – they decided who gets to make a formal presentation and they may also criticize your performance. They give preference to presenters who have a strong, clear message. (See below an example of such a message based on an innovative and thought-through strategy.)

☀ Risk-eliminating service contracts

Svedala, the Swedish-based mining and construction equipment manufacturer is offering a range of service contracts which will guarantee risk factors such as equipment performance, product quality and maintenance cost – virtually eliminating the risk in customers' operations. Svedala's manager explains their service contract strategy:

"Essentially what Svedala is offering is a performance guarantee which will optimize our customers' operations," claims Svedala's manager. "There are basically two different ways in which those customers will be able to benefit from this: firstly, there's the 'green field option', where a customer is starting up a facility, or is involved in new construction project or some kind of mining operation. Here we could even get involved in design and consultancy – the early planning stage of the plant. We could then supply much, if not all, of the equipment necessary, and can also help in providing or arranging finance for the project. The second alternative is for existing facilities, and here we would undertake a cost analysis, and an equipment analysis, and set up a scheduled maintenance program."

Svedala is offering two basic forms of service contract to provide this level of confidence to its customers. One is based on annual servicing costs and is aimed mainly at owner-operators of mobile equipment; the second is based on cost analysis and is more appropriate for the operators of mining and construction sites.

Customer benefits

The contracts are designed to benefit the customer in many different ways: "Firstly, there's an insurance-type benefit in that customers are protected against the costs of major equipment failures. Secondly, it introduces fixed costs for maintenance. If customers wish, we can even help them eliminate costs by replacing staff with Svedala employees, or by transferring existing staff to Svedala's payroll. When this happens, the customer no longer has to meet the costs associated with employing personnel (for example, training). Then the cost of vehicles and tools involved in the maintenance function could also be taken over or replaced by us under the terms of the service agreement.

Thirdly, the contract provides access to our expertise. This means that equipment can be utilized more efficiently – our knowledge and experience, in combination with our highly skilled service technicians, makes it likely that we can help the owner to get the equipment to run more efficiently and at lower cost. Also, we're better able to predict when preventative maintenance is required, thus maximizing the use of the equipment."

Quality, production, or cost guarantees

The guarantee element of the contract is flexible, based on customer needs. For example, it could be based on the quality of the product: this might appeal to an aggregate producer, where the size range of the end product is critical. Alternatively, there could be a production capacity guarantee, where production per hour within a certain range would be guaranteed or again, the guarantee could be based on the operating costs, excluding power consumption and the salaries of any customer personnel, invoiced as a fixed cost per ton produced.

The trade-off for customers is that Svedala takes over a significant part of their operations and the concomitant cost, in return for contracting all their business in spare parts and maintenance to Svedala. This proposition is available even where the capital equipment has not been bought or supplied by Svedala – the contract can be extended to competitors' plant, and will run, typically, from three to five years.

PRINCIPLES FOR PLACEMENT

The two essential principles in using the trade-press-channel are: treat editors just like other customers and treat the editorial material you produce just like the other products your company produces. The first principle requires that you anticipate the editors' needs and have the editorial product ready and waiting for them when they want it. The second principle involves taking a rational approach to the production of editorial material: making maximum use of the raw material available to you and planning the process in an effective way. Finally, as with all other products, ensuring quality and availability. These principles will be amplified in the rest of this chapter, but first I'd like to dispel a common misconception about dealing with the trade press.

By-passing the free lunch

A lot of conventional PR activity directed at influencing the trade press tends to treat it as a "black box", which has to be acted on from the outside. In other words, editors need to be manipulated into providing positive editorial coverage. The standard tools employed for this purpose are: arranged interviews, press events, and various forms of entertainment. (Even the standard press release is generally dispatched to a mass of black boxes in a spirit of spray and pray.) A far more effective approach is to convert the black box into a gateway – to prepare ready-to-publish material, written to professional trade press standards (see Figure 6.1). Editors, acting in their gate-keeper role, can then publish the material (provided its newsworthy and well-prepared) as an information service to their readers. A trade press editor once told me that, if he'd wanted to, he could have eaten lunch every working day at the expense of companies wanting to place editorial in his journal. He invariably explained to them that he didn't have the time and he'd far rather have a publishable-quality story, which would decrease his workload, than a free lunch, which would increase both the length of his working day and the circumference of his waist-line!

Collecting stamps of legitimacy

Getting through the editorial gateway gives your company's marketing messages a "stamp of legitimacy": every time an editor decides to publish something on his or her editorial pages he or she is staking the reputation of the journal on that decision.

Even the standard press release is
generally dispatched to a mass
of black boxes in a spirit of spray and pray

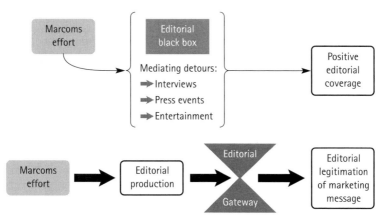

Figure 6.1 By-passing the free lunch

If your company sells its products in several different geographical and business area markets, then the global trade press can be seen as an orienteering course – the idea is to obtain as many stamps of legitimacy as possible by having your messages published in at least one relevant and reputable journal in each of your business and geographic markets.

The readership target

The idea of the "readership target" (see Figure 6.2) is to illustrate the two principle objectives for editorial placement:

- Strategic influence of decision criteria – this is one of the essential features of the case-based approach – using technology presentation articles and case stories to influence prospects and others engaged in the various stages of the B2B purchasing process. Once they have appeared in the press (and consequently acquired a stamp of legitimacy), the published versions can be used as promotional material by the sales force. The objective here is to achieve line-by-line attention from a strategic core readership of prospects and opinion leaders, such as technical experts and consultants. If they don't encounter the articles as random readers, their attention can be drawn to them by the sales force.

- Presence – this is the continual appearance of material about your company on the editorial pages of relevant trade journals. At this level – it's not necessary that the target group read the articles in any systematic way – all that's necessary is that they see that your company has been active, innovative, or newsworthy enough to get through the editorial gatekeeper. This plays a positive role in building brand loyalty.

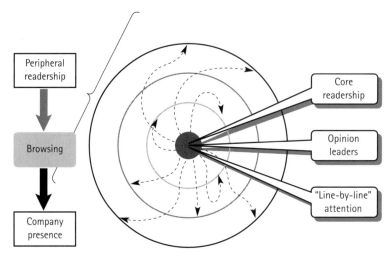

Figure 6.2 The readership target

The editorial customer

If editors are to be treated as customers it's necessary to accumulate three sets of information:

- Who are they? – the answer should be the editors of journals which serve the business and geographic markets which are most important to your company

- What do they want? – in addition to specific information on a case-to-case basis, a general answer would be good quality editorial material and pictures easily available to them at no costs in time, money, or effort

- What do they think of your company? – this can be established by "editor opinion surveys". These are designed to establish how your company is currently seen by relevant editors. A questionnaire is compiled based on how you would like to be seen. It's best applied as a blind comparison with your major competitors. (As editors are highly sophisticated market actors, this is a very cost-effective form of market research: ideally an editor should know what his/her readers think, so asking one editor should give a good idea of the attitudes of thousands of potential customers.) The results will identify a perception gap, which can then be used to guide your editorial planning.

The main points of the article
should therefore be encapsulated in
its title and introductory paragraph

The quality of the editorial product

Treating editorial material as a product means ensuring (as with all products) its quality and availability. In terms of quality, the major principle is empathize with the reader! Your material must be newsworthy, i.e. it contains something of value to the reader. The great pitfall to be avoided in editorial material produced by or on behalf of companies is company egoism. This is the delusion that customers and prospects have the same level of interest in organizational details and self-congratulation as do employees. Text should be factually informative. The benefits of a new product should not be simply presented (as might be enough in advertising copy) but some technical account of how they have been achieved should also be included. This creates the difference in credibility between editorial and advertisements.

Text should not be allowed to get too technical. Editorial in the trade press is designed to arouse interest in technical issues, not to give the sort of total explanation which might be appropriate in a scientific journal. A trade press reader who's really interested in the full technical details can contact the company directly. Material should be well written: it should have a logical, well-planned structure, be concise, and easy to understand. It's estimated that someone browsing through a magazine has an attention span of seven seconds when considering whether or not to read an article in full. The main points of the article should therefore be encapsulated in its title and introductory paragraph.

THE IDEAL CASE STORY

One excellent model for trade press editorial is the ideal case story formula (see Figure 6.3). A first piece of advice here is that, where and whenever possible, those producing the case story should meet the customer at the site where the equipment in question is being used (and take pictures of the customer in front of the equipment). This is a quality issue – the text will benefit from the writer seeing the site (and any relevant drawings, diagrams, etc.). Customers will also be more forthcoming during a person-to-person meeting and editors like personalized pictures. The actual text should be structured as follows:

- Present the customer, the nature of their business, location, size, etc. This is important in generating identification among relevant readers and provides a basis for global word-of-mouth to take place.

- Present the customer's problem – the details which led the customer to identify a need for and subsequently to buy the product in question

- Present the alternatives, in terms of both techniques and alternative suppliers (though without naming any competitors) which the customer considered

- Describe, ideally via the customer's own words, the decision criteria which he/she used to select between these alternatives

- Describe in detail how the company's products solved this problem and satisfied the customer's need, ideally with positive experiences (expressed in quantitative form) over a prolonged period.

See opposite a real-life example of the ideal case story, involving two North American farmers and their purchase of flotation tires for their very powerful tractors.

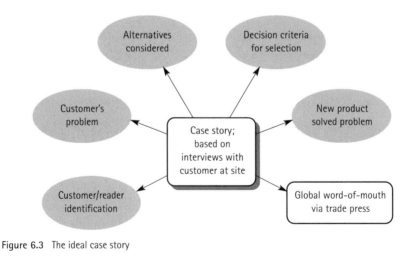

Figure 6.3 The ideal case story

☀ "Super-power" tractor problems solved by better tires

Modern, very powerful tractors enable big increases in productivity but they bring problems of slippage and soil compaction. On one North American farm a 20% productivity loss and yield reductions of 2% were cured by fitting Trelleborg tires to its powerful new tractors.

Wayne has been farming since 1949. He and his son Steve now farm 6,000 acres producing 3,000–4,000 tons of fodder crops per year plus, straw, wheat, and small grains including soybeans, which make up their biggest acreage, yielding about 30 tons per acre. Originally they used two tractors, one of 375 horse power (280 kW) and one of 400 horse power (298 kW). They both had 20.8 x 42" tires mounted in triple formation.

Wayne explains that they use a number of implements that require very effective traction such as 41 and 49 foot (12.5 and 15 meter) chisel plow, which plow to a depth of 6 to 8 inches (152–203 mm), and a sub-soiler which works to a depth of 20 inches (508 mm). They were experiencing a lot of tire slippage and Steve estimates that they were loosing about 20% of production time through this problem. The heavy tractors also caused soil compaction and Wayne believes that this problem was causing a reduction in yield of approximately 1.5 to 2% a year.

Yet more powerful tractors

Then in 1997, aiming for higher productivity, Wayne and Steve bought two 425 horse power (317 kW) John Deere 94100 tractors which have 10% boost and considerably higher torque than the two previous machines. From their experience with the tires on the old tractors, Wayne and Steve knew they were going to need some exceptional tires to cope with the very high powers produced by what are probably the most powerful tractors in the world today.

The problems explained

Three main problems have emerged with the development of very high power tractors and their associated weights. The first is slippage, which has always been present but which has become more serious with the introduction of heavy draught implements, producing (most experts believe) 10% wheel slip; this means that 10% of fuel and working time is wasted. With the high capital and running costs associated with very powerful tractors and tight margins to which agriculture is working today, 10% wheel slip makes a serious dent in profitability. In poor soil conditions, slippage may be so bad that work becomes impossible.

Soil compaction

The second problem is soil compaction caused by heavy machinery running over the land. For good growth, plants need the air and water, which is normally contained in large pores in the soil. Heavy machinery on the surface can close these pores, denying the plant what it needs to grow. Plant roots have a larger diameter than many of the soil pores so for the roots to be able to move readily through the soil, they must be able to open up these gaps. Heavily compacted soil may be too solid for them to do this so root development is restricted. To reduce compaction, the golden rule is to keep tire pressure as low as possible for the load the tires are carrying spread on the ground maximizes the footprint.

Power hopping

The third problem, which did not emerge until tractor powers broke the 250–300 horse power (186–224 kW) barrier, is power hopping. It usually occurs in tractors equipped with radial tires whose sidewalls flex or bounce under hard pulling. It is created by a resonance set up between the tires and the natural frequency of the draught of the implement. The resilience in the tires is enough for the amplitude to build up and, in severe cases, for the wheels to leave the ground.

At best, the problem is annoying and uncomfortable, at worst it's dangerous and may put undue stress on the tractor and its implement. There are a number of fixes including ballasting the tractor and increasing the air pressure in the front and/or rear tires; both these measures increase soil compaction. Changing the speed of working and changing implement working depth can also help. Rubber tracks have also been used to cure the problem. But the solution increasingly favored is replacing the tires with Trelleborg Twins which, by virtue of their size and stiff sidewalls, cure the problem without frequent pressure correction and ballast adjustments. Other manufacturers are developing larger tires which may be a solution but they have not yet stood the test of time and results are not widely known.

"We looked looked at different options for drives including four tracks," says Wayne, "but there were several things that put us off. Firstly, there was the initial cost price and secondly, the cost of track replacement. There were also the difficulties of turning. We also considered conventional triples that we had used before, but we rejected these as we had already experienced problems with them."

Steve explains that he first saw Trelleborgs at a farm show and was impressed by the product information about them. He mentions in particular the low air pressure with a flat running of the tire which uses the whole surface of the tire. They were therefore very interested to try dual mounted Trelleborg tires as another option.

"Of course, having duals both front and back was a great advantage in itself," said Steve. "It is much better to have only eight tires to consider rather than 12. When we were running the previous tractors with 12 tires we could reckon with at least three or four punctures per year. Now we have got the Trelleborgs we have only had one puncture in two years. Our main problem of slippage has disappeared and the 2% loss through soil compaction we were experiencing has gone too, now that we are using Trelleborgs."

The driving concept behind the effort to create high quality editorial is the idea of trying to counter the information chaos in which we all now live. If an editor, reader, or customer experiences your editorial material as comprehensive, digestible, quick and easy to consume, and informative and attractive then your company has achieved a competitive advantage over its competitors who fail to make the necessary effort in this area.

THE EDITORIAL PRODUCTION PROCESS

This depends, like other products, on converting raw material into a finished product (see Figure 6.4). The raw material in this case is inaccessible and/or unprocessed information from within the company. This raw material comes in two forms:

high quality editorial
counters the information chaos

in which we all now live

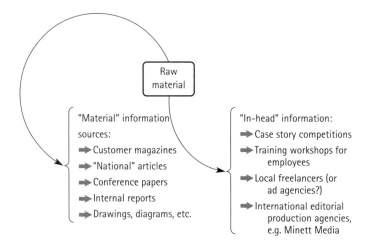

Figure 6.4 Editorial production process

"material" sources of information and "in-head" information. The material sources consist of texts which have already been produced, such as articles written for the company's customer and employee magazines, national articles (i.e. articles which may have been published about the company and its products in national journals around the world, often in languages other than English), conference papers and internal reports. These texts can be edited (translating where necessary) into trade press material. In-head is where the necessary information is in the heads of your company's personnel and/or your customers. This needs to be converted into useable editorial material.

Case story competitions

Two approaches can be proposed to solve this problem: the first is to encourage and develop the writing skills of the people who have, or are close to, the relevant knowledge. One method here is the case story competition: employees, especially salespeople, are motivated by the chance of winning significant prizes to write up their best case stories. A finesse here is to arrange for actual trade press editors to act as judges in such competitions. This has two advantages. As editors are external professionals, their judgement is likely to be perceived as fair by participating employees. Assuming that the editors' journals are relevant to your company, the competition provides an opportunity to present them with a mass of editorial material about its activities. The editors may even decide to publish one or more of the entries. Even pieces that aren't used can be edited into usable trade press material.

Another alternative is editorial training for in-house personnel. This is particularly suitable for employees who edit the company's internal and external journals – they already have writing skills and a deep knowledge of your company and its products and it's usually easier for them to get hold of relevant people and information. Therefore, equipping them with trade-press skills can increase the volume and quality of your editorial production. The other approach is to use external writers and agencies to write your material from scratch. On a national level, the alternatives are generally local freelancers or advertising agencies. In terms of cost-effectiveness, a good local freelancer with whom you can build up a long-term relationship is probably the best bet. The multi-usage of editorial material does, of course, work both ways, so that once material has been created for the trade press it can then also be used in the company's own journals (internal and external), annual reports, brochures, websites, advertorials, etc.

Making editorial products available

In implementing the availability principle, the advice (once again) is to treat editorial in the same way as any other product. The pitfall to avoid here is the reactive approach, which consists of waiting for editors to ring up asking for editorial contributions and then frantically rushing around trying to put together something appropriate to send them. (A company should certainly not be doing this with any other customer nor any other product.)

treat editorial in the same way
as any other product

Using editorial material as a marketing tool requires planning its production well in advance, and having pre-prepared material ready for when your target journals have appropriate editorial themes. Your production planning can be guided by a number of simple questions:

- what are the most significant things your company is currently doing in all your major business and geographic markets?

- what major projects is your company currently involved in?

- what are your new products and star products and how are they being used?

Applying case-analysis

The case analysis procedure (as described in Chapter Two) should also be applied in your editorial planning. This involves B2B marketers carrying out analyses of all the available sales processes (successful and unsuccessful) of the products for which they are responsible. One of the objectives of this is to identify trends and patterns in prospects' decision criteria. Having established these, successful companies will then present effectively differentiated solutions capable of fulfilling these criteria. In advanced contemporary societies two very characteristic patterns of customer criteria cluster around environmental and health concerns. Here are examples of two cases which, respectively, address these concerns.

Advanced recycling system solves city's sludge disposal problem

A city in Northern Europe will be a pioneer in the field of domestic sludge disposal by adopting Kemwater's "KREPRO" process. This will provide the city with a stable, reliable, and long-term sludge disposal solution. A solution, moreover, which can largely satisfy media and other critics regarding the environmental safety of the city's sludge disposal process.

The city is subject to very stringent standards regarding the content of sludge to be used on farmland. The technical director of the city's water company states that, "We have been meeting these standards since the

1970s; there's been a considerable decrease of heavy metals in our sludge. It's now at such a low level that it's very difficult to reduce it further because there are only a few and very small point sources left. Most of the minimal heavy metal contamination that's left comes from diffuse sources like atmospheric fall-out, presence in different products used in households, presence in food, etc. For this reason, the heavy metal content in sludge can never be zero. The remaining sources are small and are slowly decreasing. The metal concentrations are well within our national limits, which are themselves below EU limits imposed in the 1980s. As a result, our government still requires the nation's water companies to recycle a proportion of their sewage sludge as an agricultural fertilizer."

Environmental opposition

A new force in the issue of sludge disposal has been the rise of the very powerful environmental lobby, consisting of non-governmental green organizations and spokespeople. These groups have had a powerful influence on food producers. As a result of these debates, the public has become extremely knowledgeable and sensitive about any possible contaminants in sludge used as fertilizer: for example, three topics came up at the end of 1999: firstly, objection was raised to the chemical used for flame retardant in furniture, which is contaminating sludge. Secondly, the national environmental agency included silver among the items to be monitored in sludge. Thirdly, there was a claim that pathogenic bacteria are ending up in the finished sludge product for fertilizer because there is no pasteurization of the sludge to ensure that they are killed off.

As a result of this type of campaigning, the farmers' union made a decision not to accept sludge from sewage treatment plants as fertilizers. They recommend their members not to take sludge on farming land. Buyers of crops have also decided on new policies against sludge; they don't want to buy products coming from land which has been fertilized by sludge. All this, of course, had the effect of intensifying the search for more satisfactory ways of disposing of, and ideally recycling sludge, especially given the fact that this is required by the Government.

Options for disposal

The technical director reviews the various disposal options: "Firstly, there's use on farmland: Stringent standards are applied here and we're making continuous improvements. What's needed is a system for sludge handling which follows all the rules and which can generate widespread social acceptance. This leaves, the use of sludge in topsoil, by mixing with sand and composting. The problems here are limited demand, where it's easy to find natural topsoil. This method is also vulnerable to the same arguments against the direct use of sludge on farmland. Secondly, there's landfill, currently the commonest method. However, this option is rapidly disappearing – permits are impossible to obtain, landfill sites are more or less impossible to find and it will not be permitted after 2005. Finally, incineration; co-incineration with other forms of waste is an interesting alternative. But again, no permits have been granted, not very many plants are equipped for it and there may be capacity problems. There will certainly also be high requirements on air emissions."

The KREPRO solution

The city's water company studied the options available for sludge disposal and decided to adopt the Kemwater's KREPRO process as the solution which would come closest to answering the problems facing the company. The technical director concludes that, "the main factor influencing the decision has been that it provides an environmentally acceptable solution to the disposal problem. It's also, clearly, a bonus if the costs can be kept no higher than they are at present. The KREPRO process is the only more or less pure phosphorous recycling alternative which produces a product equivalent to commercial fertilizers – and the pilot plant in Helsingborg has demonstrated that the process works" he adds.

This second case example deals with a growing health care problem in modern hospitals.

Managing latex sensitization in infection control

Latex is the optimal material for medical gloves. However, it's now clear that prolonged skin contact with latex can lead to sensitization symptoms, which in susceptible individuals can be very severe. Helped by a glove-use audit from Healthline (a glove manufacturer), an English hospital is managing this problem with an appropriate glove-use policy.

By the late 1960s and early 1970s, gloves were being introduced for more and more activities on hospital wards. The problem of latex sensitization actually emerged in the early to mid-1980s, and arises from long-term intimate skin contact with latex – which can take many years to develop. It was a hidden problem both in the sense that the symptoms took time to manifest and also there was a lack of recognition of the symptoms, which could include chapping of the skin, dryness or soreness, itchiness and even cracks in the skin, and bleeding.

Referrals to dermatologists for advice on latex sensitization developed in the late 1980s and early 1990s, where it became recognized as a condition associated with latex contact. The condition is an allergic reaction with two possible explanations. Firstly, it is thought to be a reaction to the proteins in latex. The use of powders on gloves – which make them easier to put on and take off – actually promotes the latex sensitization because the proteins tend to adhere to the powder which makes contact with the skin easier. Secondly, the chemicals used in the manufacture of latex gloves may also be a factor. People who are predisposed to allergies are most vulnerable. In the worst case, reaction can result in analphactic shock which can even lead to death. There have almost certainly been fatal cases of latex sensitization in the UK, though it is difficult to provide figures as some earlier cases will almost certainly have been misdiagnosed.

And yet, there is no question that latex does appear to be the best protection against pathogenic organisms which may be present in blood and other body fluids – and this claim has been tested by use for over 100 years. Latex has many desirable features: it has very good surface tension, so fits very well and is very flexible, and in many cases can reseal after having been punctured. Compared with possible alternatives, such as vinyl and plastic, it is known that certain pathogenic organisms can actually pass through these while they cannot pass through latex. Also these materials lack the flexibility of latex, they are more easily split, exposing clinical personnel to the risk of any pathogens the gloves are designed to protect against.

The latex dilemma

"The dilemma then, from an infection control point of view, is that the wearing of glove protection became more and more desirable, especially after the advent of HIV, while at the same time the problem of latex sensitization was also increasing," says the infection control specialist. A further point is that some latex gloves are more expensive than other gloves, and by the mid-1990s, cost pressures on the National Health Service had become a significant factor. The use of gloves at this hospital increased 30% in the year 1995 alone as clinical staff were advised that "protecting yourself is protecting the patient", though this obviously impacted on budgets.

Finding solutions

Part of the effort to solve the latex sensitization dilemma comes from changes in the materials and manufacture of latex gloves. Healthline is a company which manufactures and markets a range of gloves and other medical disposable items. Their representative at the hospital is also a qualified and former working nurse (in line with that company's policy for its representatives). She says, "One of the first steps to counter sensitization was the introduction and wide spread use of powder free latex gloves. This helps to reduce the distribution of latex proteins. We are now introducing polymer-coated gloves and texture coated latex gloves and can offer a wide range of powder free latex gloves. We are also introducing nitrile gloves made from a synthetic rubber which provide a barrier to pathogenic organisms almost as effective as latex, but without the latex sensitization problem."

But the hospital's infection control specialist refers to the link that hospitals have to make between the problem of latex sensitization and their cost pressures. "This gives them one choice," she says, "and that is the strategy of appropriate use – to ensure that people know what gloves to use for any clinical or invasive procedure, and also when it is not appropriate to use gloves at all, to avoid over-use. This is arguably the most sensible rational strategy for hospitals to adopt."

Glove-use audit

The first step in adopting an appropriate use strategy is to carry out an audit of what gloves are used in a hospital, what sort of procedures they are used for, and how knowledgeable people are about which gloves are appropriate for what type of activity. Healthline offered to carry out such an audit. The infection control specialist comments: "We were delighted to have this audit done by Healthline having limited time, and especially finance, to undertake it ourselves. It was also valuable to have a fresh eye, especially a former nurse, looking at the situation in the hospital. Arguably too, she has been able to get more honest responses than might ourselves."

The audit included a review of what type of gloves (i.e. of what material, whether they were powdered or not, etc.) were in use in the hospital; whether the use of those particular gloves were appropriate for the activities they were being used for; whether there were any problems with the gloves; how aware personnel were about the hospital policy on glove use; and a number of questions to individuals about their own experiences of latex sensitivity.

In addition to the audit, Healthline also made their representative available (at the company's expense) to the hospital as a training resource. All members of staff have statutory training each year in infection control and the Healthline training can be integrated into other programs to discuss the more appropriate use of gloves. This training is important, given that there are approximately 40 independent purchasers of gloves within the hospital, with each department, ward, and team purchasing its own gloves independently of each other, and from separate budgets. Despite this, Healthline supplies some 80% of the gloves used at the hospital.

The objectives in both these cases are: firstly, to carefully define the customers' problems, within their full socio-economic and technical contexts. (It will be recalled that just these problems have been strategically selected from the companies' case analyses, as being currently characteristic for their respective target organizations, i.e. water service companies and general hospitals.) Then, secondly, to offer an acceptable solution, which (both companies being pioneers in their respective fields) effectively differentiates your company from its competitors.

Approval

Another factor in product availability concerns making material ready to use quickly and effectively. A major problem here can be getting approval of texts. This can be considered from both the internal and the external point of view (external meaning case stories, where it's necessary to get approval from one of your company's customers). Internally, there are two pitfalls to avoid; the technical and the bureaucratic. In the first there is a danger of becoming obsessive about technical correctness. If certain technical points are too complicated to be comfortably explained in trade press material, then merely refer to them without explanation or simply leave them out. (Trade journals differ from scientific journals in not requiring total explanations.) Obsessiveness of an even less justifiable kind is often exercised over trivial factual references: what is the precisely correct legal name of a company? What is the exact distance between one town and another? Who decided what in the history of the company over the last 20 years? The guide to cutting a way through all such issues is the question "Will this be of interest to the trade press reader?" If the answer is no, then keep it simple or leave it out.

The bureaucratic pitfall concerns responsibilities for approving texts; the larger the group involved and the more vaguely defined these responsibilities are, the more difficulties and delays in getting approval. Ideally one individual within the company should have overall responsibility for approving trade press texts. Naturally, he or she should be open to editorial input from all colleagues who may have an interest in the text, but by applying the guidelines above he or she can ensure that approval is achieved quickly and effectively. This may require centralizing the management of this task and steps should be taken to avoid "turf" divisions within companies and multi-national groups, e.g. between: national and

keep it simple or

leave it out.

international units, corporate communications departments and marketing departments, sales and marketing, etc. In tackling external approval, where for example a customer needs to approve a case story about their plant or organization, a good strategy is to emphasize that publication will provide valuable positive publicity for their organization at zero cost to them.

Promoting product awareness

Again as with other products, having produced it, the next step is to create product awareness. A first priority should be to do this within your own company. The objective here is to get your own people to see the value of editorial activity and therefore be willing to provide information and approval quickly and effectively. My agency uses three methods to promote editorial material to the trade press:

- Reports to journals. These consist of information promoting articles which our clients have commissioned us to get published. The information consists of the title of the article, its introductory paragraph and the number of words in the complete text of the article. Editors can then download from our site or request from us the full text of the articles in which they're interested.

- Article promotion website. This functions in a similar way to the reports; the same promotional information about each article is available and editors can down-load the full text direct from the site. The main difference is that for the reports we select a list of suitable articles based on business areas, while the website has information on all our articles currently available for publication and the editors themselves select which they are interested in via a menu of business areas. This site is, in effect, a "B2B article exchange."

- Teleplacement. This service is directed at each client's "premier list" of journals. For these we first identify an appropriate slot for the articles in the journal's editorial calendar, then call, or email, the editor to encourage their publication.

Global or local placement?

For companies which engage in extensive international marketing, the question of local versus global distribution of feature articles for the trade press is often considered within the wider context of its policy on marketing as a whole. If the company tends to favor a local rather than global approach to marketing, then (presumably in the interests of consistency) this policy is often, unreflectingly, applied also to this placement activity. Having had wide experience in this particular area, I'm convinced that this is a mistake for the following reasons.

Knowledge of press plus placement effort

For very obvious reasons, when asked (for example, at the company's global marketing conferences) local companies will invariably say that they "know" their local trade press and are actively placing material in it. The reality, however, is likely to be very different, simply because it takes time, manpower, and resources to:

- keep track of the trade press
- get their attention for the material you have to offer
- deal with questions about text and pictures and ensure that they get them by their publication deadlines
- obtaining copies of published material.

Many local companies are exclusively sales companies and are judged on their sales results. Consequently, they are reluctant to devote their limited resources to other activities. (Despite the effectiveness of a case-based approach to B2B marketing many companies do not keep or even ask about statistics on editorial placements.)

Global placement (either managed internally or sub-contracted to a specialist global placement agency) ensures exclusive focus on achieving the four objectives above and on reporting detailed progress in this area to the global organization as a whole.

A few local companies may be doing a reasonable placement job, but most will be doing very little or nothing. (If you doubt this, ask for physical evidence of the publications achieved – copies or at least journal titles, dates of publication, etc.) Global placement (especially by an agency) works because editors around the world learn to come to one center to get material about one or more international companies. By doing this, they clearly demonstrate that they are not getting material from the local sales organizations (for the reasons given above).

Global placement does not in any way interfere with personal relations between local company and local press – in fact it can improve them. If editors are being efficiently served with the material they want about your company from a global center, which ensures that it's properly prepared and delivered on time, the local personnel are relieved of this mechanical part of the job. They can then concentrate on the personal side of the relationship – which can sour if the mechanical part is done badly or not at all.

Apart from efficiency issues, there's also the question of sharing the results of publication efforts. If article placement is left entirely to the local level, then that's more than likely where the results will stay. Editors these days generally see the world as borderless. The idea that each country's case stories must be kept exclusively within that country may appeal to those who run local companies but the publication record of agencies such as mine shows that this view is no longer shared (if it ever was) by editors – neither is it in the interests of their readers and your potential customers.

If the global placement service obtains physical copies of published articles, they then become (at least potentially) available to the Group worldwide, enabling your sales force to draw on an enormous stock of presentations and case stories bearing the stamp of legitimacy of publication.

SUMMARY: CREATING AND SWEATING EDITORIAL ASSETS

For B2B marketers pursuing a case-based approach, trade press editorial can be seen as *the* public arena in which to engage in rational discourse about their products and services. Their goals in this area should, therefore, be to maximize:

- production of relevant and publishable material
- its publication in appropriate trade journals
- utilization by the sales force of the company's published material.

In the production phase, the objective is to generate and maintain a "portfolio" of highly effective strategic articles. These should be regularly reviewed with regard to the relevance of their messages. The task then is to maximize the publication of

the objective is
to generate and maintain
a "portfolio" of highly effective
strategic articles

this material in relevant trade journals and, having done so, to maximize the availability of relevant published material to the company's sales force. The two essential principles for achieving this are: treat trade press editors just like any other customer of your company and treat the editorial material you produce just like the other products which your company produces and sells. The first principle requires that you anticipate the editors' needs and have the editorial product ready and waiting for them when they want it. The second principle involves taking a rational approach to the production of editorial material; making maximum use of the raw material available to you and planning the process in an effective way. Finally, as with all other products, ensure quality and availability.

Implementing these principles provides many opportunities for feedback and organizational learning. Ideally the results of establishing and operating the system will lead to a change in organizational attitudes, culture, and behavior, enabling the company to become a "case-oriented" organization. Externally, the result should be "presence" and impact for the company in the world's trade press, plus a rich source of highly effective sales material.

chapter seven

CASE-BASED

COMMUNICATIONS

As stated in Chapter Two, one of the central ideas of case-based marketing is to use an analysis of existing cases to guide the marketing communications (marcoms) effort. A consummate practitioner of this art is Björn von Euler, Director of Corporate Communications at ITT Fluid Technology. He recalls the early days of the method, when he and I were working together in Stockholm: "I started working seriously with case stories in 1988. This was when Steve Minett moved from the head office of Atlas Copco to the head office of ITT Flygt, where I was then Marketing Communications manager. Together, we started to use case stories as the focal thrust of our marcoms strategy. This method has many advantages:

- it provides a clear focus for the production of material, especially where cases are being produced for an in-house journal

- to attract attention you have to be interesting: cases can do this and "tell our story", in a way that other forms of promotional material can't. The information in a case can be useful to the audience, plus they can personally identify with it. Cases can be both local and global

- it's cost-effective – you have a one-off investment for each case; establishing the contacts, getting the best pictures, ideally dramatic, and preparing the best quality text

- it's very flexible – the same case can be edited to address many audiences: highly technical articles for specifying engineers, journalistic pieces for the financial community, simpler stories for the general public, etc. – you can even talk to friends about a case!

- cases can be communicated via different media: the trade press, in-house journals, websites, advertisements, videos – even events and speeches. For example, we often refer to our current contributions to the Olympics or our contributions to major world projects such as the Channel Tunnel, it's very effective to use these references when world attention is focussed on them.

I'd have to say that for the B2B marketer, a case-based communications strategy is simply the best available option." In this chapter we'll consider how to structure cases for placement in response to market feedback and look at a number of real-life examples.

INFLUENCING MARKET OPINION VIA CASE-BASED PROMOTION

What case analysis (as per the model in Chapter Two) can provide is feedback on prospects' reactions to your product during actual sales processes. As we have seen, prospects may be at different stages of the sales process. Rackham suggests a whole gamut of strategies which salespeople can use to influence prospects, depending on where they are in the sales process and what positions they have adopted. For marcoms purposes, these strategies can be divided into two basic groups: "Pedagogic," where sales feedback indicates lack of knowledge of the product and/or its characteristics and "Advocacy," where sales feedback indicates that there are established objections, or preferred alternatives, to the product (see Figure 7.1). For the rest of this chapter we'll move clockwise around this cluster of "persuasion strategies," looking at the nature of each strategy, when it should be applied and examine a real-life example, in the form of a case story or technology presentation article.

The pedagogic presentation of need

The sales force may have discovered that there is very little perceived need for the product. In this case, just as Rackham advises for a salesperson, the marcom message targeted at potential customers should aim to uncover and intensify the need which the product can satisfy. Uncover here means to encourage prospects to perceive a need where they may not have perceived one before. Such needs often arise out of new trends in society, e.g. concerns over the environment and employee health and safety. The example on pages 176–7 relates to the environmental issue of disposing of redundant computers.

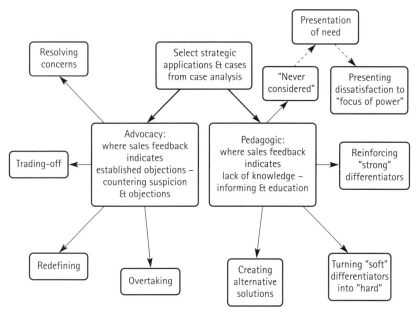

Figure 7.1 Presenting strategic applications and cases

Recycling might be an issue of which computer manufacturers are only vaguely aware. The objective in this piece is to reverse their probable assumption that while recycling might enhance their image, it would entail a significant financial cost. Pointing out that they can get this marketing advantage, plus guarding against piracy and being ahead of the legislation, while at the same time making a profit removes any obstacles to perceiving recycling as a "need-to-do" activity.

these strategies can be divided into two basic groups:

"Pedagogic,"

where sales feedback indicates lack of knowledge of the product and/or its characteristics and

"Advocacy,"

where sales feedback indicates that there are established objections, or preferred alternatives, to the product

Recycling computers: Boliden's concept

As with cars, the totally recyclable computer is a desirable concept from many perspectives; environmentally, commercially, and from a marketing point of view. Boliden, with a long tradition of handling non-ferrous metals, has come up with a totally inclusive process. In addition to being impeccably green, the process provides computer manufacturers with guarantees against component pirating and a financial surplus from each machine processed.

Conventionally, computer manufacturers have not had any effective system available for recycling their products. In the best case scenario, computers may be sold to back-street scrap merchants who will take out the precious metals and dump the rest of the equipment. The majority end up in landfill sites. This is not a very satisfactory state of affairs: disposal in landfill sites creates a risk of heavy metal contamination, which not only damage the environment but can also pose a risk to human health. The head of Boliden's recycling business area comments, "The law is being used more and more in these areas. Within the near future most industrial countries will almost certainly introduce taxes on the disposal of environmentally sensitive materials such as the heavy metals used in computers."

Component pirating

The alternative of disposal via the traditional, small-scale, scrap industry is not much better. Environmentally, these operators are not very reliable. Secondly, the dispersed structure of the traditional scrap industry can pose a threat to the reputation and brand integrity of computer manufacturers: the issue here is the unauthorized reuse of components such as microchips and circuit boards. If these turn up in the machines of smaller manufacturers, selling to the lower end of the computer market, they could cause problems for the original manufacturers of the components.

Guarantees against pirating

Boliden is offering computer manufacturers a partnership relationship in a total computer recycling process. "We can adopt this strategy," says a Boliden spokesperson, "because we have a totally integrated operation in this business area. No middle men are involved." Boliden has a long tradition in smelting non-ferrous metals and in Scandinavia, where the company's approach to computer recycling is most developed, Boliden has its own scrap yards. "We can keep the entire process under our control. For example, we can give guarantees that components will in fact be recycled rather than disappearing out the back door and falling into the hands of pirates."

Not only green – profitable

There are also financial advantages: personal computers can contain up to $200 worth of precious metals. Consequently, dumping them in landfills is not only environmentally irresponsible, it's also financially wasteful. The value of the precious metals not only pays for the entire recycling process but normally provides a surplus which is returned to the computer manufacturer. The manufacturer also gets the value of any reusable components that can be retrieved.

Marketing edge

The marketing implications provide another commercial incentive. In the same way as car manufacturers, computer makers can start using the recyclability of their products in their marketing strategies as part of their brand identity. Taking this approach now has two advantages for manufacturers: firstly, it raises their reputation among green-oriented consumers – arguably a majority of the computer buying public. Secondly, it means they'll be a step ahead when, as is virtually certain, environmental legislation in this area is introduced.

Reinforcing strong criteria

When the sale enters the evaluation of options stage, prospects' decision criteria begin to emerge. The task then is to influence the formation of these criteria in order to maximize the fit between them and your product's differentiators.

Rackham suggests that when a salesperson encounters a prospect whose top priority decision criteria fit almost perfectly with the differentiators of the product he/she is offering, the salesperson's task is simply to reinforce this linkage. In marcoms terms this could be where case analysis reveals that your product has clear advantages for its potential customers' applications, but that they have little knowledge about its existence and characteristics. The marcoms task is then to pedagogically inform about, and reinforce, this linkage. The example here concerns a dynamic sand-bed filter at an environmentally well-managed steel plant.

A steel plant case: avoiding clogging with continuous sand filters

A major steel plant in Northern Europe has recently installed a new rolling mill. In conjunction with this, they've introduced the principle of 100% recycling of both the process water and slag resulting from the cooling process. As part of their effort to implement this, they've installed a DynaSand filtration plant. They now take in less water than they did before they built the new mill and the water they discharge is cleaner than the river water they take in. In addition, they have no clogging problems in the thousands of nozzles used in their low-pressure cooling system.

Why DynaSand?

When asked why the plant decided to install a DynaSand water filtration plant, the Project Leader for the water treatment plant for the new mill, explained that: "We had two main motivations. First and foremost was our environmental policy: with the establishment of our new mill, we introduced the principle of 100% recycling. This means that our goal is to recycle all the cooling water and all the slag produced by the cooling process. Consequently, following cooling we have to separate the slag from the water, clean the water for reuse and return the slag to the blast furnace, where it is an excellent raw material."

"Our second motivation was purely technical. The cooling water we use needs to be of a very high standard of purity. This is because we use an advanced cooling system which requires very clean water: the equipment consists of 37,000 nozzles, with a diameter of approximately 4 mm and about 100 mm in length. Water is discharged through these nozzles under very low pressure, just gravity, more or less. The nozzles can easily become blocked, especially because of the very low pressure." The minimum requirements for water quality for this process are: less than 10 mg of suspended solids per liter and the content of oil or grease should be under 2 mg per liter. (Oil and grease tend to leak into the cooling water from the rolling mills' lubrication systems.) The plant's cooling stages requires up to 15,000 m^3 of water per hour.

"We installed 20 DynaSand units," explains Waterlink's representative for the steel plant. "All of the units are in continuous operation 24 hours a day. Precipitation is brought about inside the DynaSand units by adding a chemical coagulant, polyaluminium chloride. The function of this coagulant is to form flocs from the oil and finer particles." The coagulant is added at the inlet to the DynaSand units and then the flocs are filtered out by the DynaSand's sandbed. As regards the performance of the DynaSand units, the suspended solid content of the filtered water is down to around 5 mg per liter and the oil and grease content is also significantly reduced. No clogging of the cooling system has occurred since the installation of the DynaSand units.

(DynaSand is known in the US under the name Supersand Continuous Sand Filter.)

The key point in this case is the need to use recycled water in the plant's advanced cooling system, while avoiding the clogging of the system's micro nozzles. The DynaSand filter could adequately meet these requirements, whereas alternative solutions couldn't. This makes it a "killer application"[1] in terms of filtration equipment for other steel plants, around the world, using this advanced cooling system in combination with recycled water.

More commonly, B2B marcoms has to address two more difficult tasks. Informing and educating, and countering suspicion and objections. The first of these marcoms role is necessary where case analysis indicates a lack of awareness of, attention to, or interest in, particular product benefits in which your product is strong. Either prospects simply haven't thought about relevant differentiators or salespeople are encountering prospects who don't understand the product's soft differentiators. The first example, concerning unthought-of differentiators, deals with the use of a waste product as a raw material – a situation which most manufacturers would not associate with quality and special benefits.

Waste product perfect for flooring

A market leader in flooring is using alumino-silicate micro-spheres, which form spontaneously when coal is burnt in power plants, to improve the quality of its flooring materials.

Fillite is a material that occurs in fuel residue from coal-fired power plants. (Prior to the 1960s, this was regarded entirely as a waste product.) About 1% of the residue consists of "cenospheres", i.e. spherical alumino-silicate micro spheres which are air-filled and occur in various sizes. They form spontaneously when coal is burnt in power plants. Cenospheres float to the surface when fly ash is pumped into ponds. Research indicated that they had properties which could only be duplicated by very expensively produced synthetic materials. In order to exploit the potential of this waste material, the Fillite company was founded in 1969. It's now owned by Trelleborg and is dedicated to finding applications for these cenospheres.

Fillite's flooring advantages

A spokesperson for a flooring company, which now uses Fillite, points out that the material has a number of advantages as a filling material in flooring products. "One of the most important is its low specific gravity, 0.65 to 0.85 g/cm^3. The PVC plastisol material we use has a specific gravity of between 1.3 and 1.5 g/cm^3. When the Fillite is added, its specific gravity may be reduced to 1.1 g/cm^3. This means that, if we use Fillite as a filler, our flooring may weigh, for example, 2.6 kg/m^2, but if we use a solid- mineral particle filler, which in some lines is the alternative, the weight may be more than 3 kg/m^2. This matters because we're looking for a quality we describe as 'heft,' which means maximum substance combined with optimum weight. This gives a good impression of the product to the customer."

A second Fillite advantage is impact resistance, i.e. the avoidance of mechanical damage to the floor when things are dropped onto it. "The spheres are very strong and won't break. If something is dropped onto the floor, the plastic material will absorb the impact while the spheres will help to retain the original shape. Another advantage is acoustics, the flooring company recently developed a sound-damping flooring material. Their head of research affirms that the sound dampening qualities of Fillite were advantageous in this flooring. A fourth, and perhaps more superficial, advantage is the color of the Fillite material, which is gray. Market research indicates customers tend to prefer gray on the underside of flooring.

"From our point of view," comments the flooring researcher, "the only alternative to Fillite is solid, mineral particle filler. This would result in flooring products which would generally be too heavy. The weight would make it floppy when handled – again, a source of negative customer perception. Also, in terms of its physical properties, it is less resistant to impact – for example, when items are dropped onto the kitchen floor. This may result in permanent damage, rather than the resilient return to shape of a structure utilizing Fillite. On the issue of weight of the mineral particle, there's also the question of shipping and handling – obviously, the heavier the product, the more (relatively) costly and difficult these activities will be."

The task this message can achieve is to get other manufacturers (of flooring and other products) to consider the characteristics of Fillite – a material which they may never have heard about.

Making soft differentiators hard

One method to harden up soft differentiators is to have their benefits pointed out by objective authorities in the field. This interview with two university researchers helped to promote ITT Flygt's "race track" design for waste water plants, which uses fine-bubble membrane diffusers and is mainly installed to assist "denitrification" (i.e. the removal of nitrates from waste water before discharge into the environment).

☀ The optimal conditions for aeration – the views of two leading researchers

Both these researchers work at a European institute for water treatment research. They have achieved an international reputation in the field of oxygen transfer efficiency. In this interview they discuss the implications of their research for the water industry, looking specifically at selecting the optimum conditions for aeration processes.

Mechanical aerators vs diffusers?

Question: On the basis of your research, could you please give your views on the various merits of the following types of aeration equipment design, with special reference to the efficiency of:
a) mechanical surface aerators b) coarse-bubble diffusers c) fine-bubble diffusers?

Researcher One: In the case of mechanical surface aerators, oxygen absorption depends partly on water droplets forming in air and partly on air bubbles under water. Water droplets in air provide less efficient oxygen transfer than air bubbles under water. In addition, the bubbles generated by mechanical aerators initially have a downward velocity, which is good for transfer. However, this soon reverses and they start to travel towards the surface, but, by then, they have lost most of their oxygen.

With air diffusion systems, oxygen transfer takes place via the interface of the bubble with the water. The greater this surface area is, in relation to the bubble's volume, the more rapid the oxygen transfer will be. Since the surface area of a bubble is proportional to the square of its diameter and the volume to its cube, the rate of transfer is inversely proportional to the diameter of the bubble. For example, a coarse bubble which is three times larger than a fine bubble, has an interface which is, proportionally, only one-third that of the fine bubble. In addition, fine bubbles rise at a slower rate than coarse bubbles. For both these reasons, fine bubbles are more efficient at transferring oxygen than coarse bubbles.

Synthetic rubber membrane versus ceramic

Question: What are the optimal materials for the manufacture of diffusers, with special regard to the choice of membrane or ceramic forms?

Researcher Two: The membrane diffuser is much better suited to the stop-start aeration cycle required for nitrification and denitrification, and the amount of nitrification and denitrification being carried out is increasing.

"Race-tracks"

Question: So-called "race-track" systems, i.e. a combination of fine bubble diffusers and artificially induced horizontal flow, are now being installed. What are your experiences of such systems?

Researcher One: One of the main intentions behind a "race-track" design is to increase bubble retention time. However, simply shifting the stream of bubbles, together with the surrounding water, sideways does not have much beneficial effect on oxygen transfer: what's necessary for this is to renew the interface between bubble and water. In other words, the bubbles have to move through the water, rather than being moved with it. A race-track affects this by shifting the bubbles out of the upward currents generated by the diffusers. This effect does slow, to some extent, the rise of the bubbles and, consequently has some beneficial effect on transfer.

Researcher Two: The main advantage of the race-track plant design is in denitrification. Because it ensures a constant process flow in the plant, it simplifies the engineering and the operations necessary to carry out the denitrification process. While race-tracks are slightly more efficient for aeration, this is a minor consideration. They're mainly selected because of their advantages for denitrification.

As was known beforehand, the empirical work that they had done in this area had clearly convinced these two researchers that fine-bubble, membrane diffusers in a race-track configuration represents the best solution for denitrification. Getting these opinions published clearly gave ITT's salespeople a tool to harden the soft differentiators of their system alternative.

Creating alternative solutions

This strategy requires the presentation of solutions of which customers were completely unaware, to the extent that they hadn't included them in their original list of options. The first example concerns lake pollution in Japan.

A mechanical solution for a case of lake pollution in Japan

Submersible mixers, carrying out artificial respiration, have saved a Japanese golf club from a very nasty pollution problem. Its scenic, artificial lakes were overgrown with weeds and algae – and producing a very unfashionable smell. The mixers have restored the water in the lakes to a fresh, natural condition.

Artificial lakes

Nine artificial lakes are distributed around the club's course. About four years after the opening, however, the lakes began accumulating a thick sediment, containing washed-off fertilizers from the surrounding lawns. This accumulation of organic matter led to a tremendous growth of vegetation and algae. The enormous increase of organic material threatened the lake's biological balance: bacteria at the bottom of lakes, which digest organic compounds, consume oxygen during the process. As the quantity of organic material increased, so did the populations of these bacteria and, consequently, the amount of oxygen which they extracted from the water. The oxygen content of the water became severely depleted, resulting in unhealthy and unsightly conditions in the lakes. Anaerobic bacterial activity produced an excess of methane (hydrogen sulfide) gas, which rose to the surface giving off an unpleasant smell.

Manual cleaning inadequate

The green keepers initially tried manual cleaning. The lakes were dragged and the bottom vegetation was cut. The loosened vegetable debris was then hauled out of the lakes. This manual approach, however, proved to be inadequate for the scale of the problem. A number of alternative water purification methods were considered including chemical stabilization, filtration, ultra violet rays, and the ozone method. None of these was ever seriously contemplated, however, because of the excessive running and maintenance costs which they all would have involved.

Enter Flygt Japan

Finally, ITT Flygt Japan was called in. They set up field trials with one submersible mixer in an attempt to use Flygt's artificial respiration system to stimulate the oxygen content of these lakes (see page 19). This trial was highly successful. There was no eutrophication of waters in the lake where it operated the following summer and no appearance of algae and bottom vegetation. This has not re-appeared during the following four years. In addition, the sludge visible at the bottom of the lake has turned from a gray color to a more natural brown and yellow coloration. As a result of this successful experience the club has now purchased a total of 102 Flygt submersible mixers. These are distributed around the club's lakes, with 10 to 12 mixers installed in each lake.

This innovative mechanical method provided an unexpected solution to a problem which seriously threatened the club's business.

CASE-BASED MARCOMS AS ADVOCACY: COUNTERING SUSPICIONS AND OBJECTIONS

This more demanding marcoms task is required where case analysis reveals that prospects either *have thought* about your product's relevant differentiators and then discarded them, or value other differentiators – in which your product is weak – above those in which your product is strong. (As always in case analysis, *both* successful and unsuccessful sales cases should be considered when determining this.) We've taken four of Rackham's tactics in this area:

- overtaking

- redefining

- trading-off, and

- resolving concerns.

Here, direct mapping from sales strategy to marcoms strategy becomes less closely coupled. (We've put alternative solutions in Pedagogics. After all, a sales meeting is a two-way conversation whereas most marcoms channels are one-way only.) In this context they all rely on the presentation of arguments and evidence to overcome pre-established opinions – this can certainly be done using marcoms messages.

Discarded incidental differentiators

In the first situation prospects may have heard about and thought about certain differentiators as potential solutions to their problems, but dismissed them as non-viable. The first example, on page 187, concerns a steel-rubber laminate for noise dampening.

The task in this piece is to introduce the idea that Trelleborg's patented bonding system has really succeeded in creating a laminate which can be worked into components like ordinary metal, contrary to the conventional wisdom, which was based on previous failed attempts.

Overtaking

The overtaking strategy should be employed where case analysis indicates that one particular differentiator (in terms of which your product is not strong) seems to be

A steel-rubber laminate that can quieten cars and other machines

Sound damping in cars and other machines has up to now tended to be an add-on extra which falls off easily and absorbs dirt and grease. Trelleborg Rubore has now developed a steel-rubber laminate material which absorbs noise and vibration which can be built into cars or machines during assembly.

The nature of the new material

The materials are called Duru-Lam and consist of a sandwich of, usually, nitrile rubber between sheets of a metal, usually steel. The secret of the success of the materials is the patented bonding process which ensures that the constituents do not separate under harsh conditions. This ensures that Duru-Lam materials can be worked, just like plain sheet, into components – automotive oil pans, transmission covers, motor mounts, steering brackets, door latches, brake covers, etc. "The material handles just like normal steel, except that our materials are acoustically dead in comparison to solid materials," says Rubore's President. "Because the layers are vulcanized together they are impossible to separate, therefore there is no problem with deep drawing which means that existing machine tools can be used to manufacture components."

There have been previous attempts to produce a sound-absorbing sandwich but these have not always come up to expectations. "The alternative has been to try and use adhesive/steel composites or visco-elastic material. However, it's not really practical for this purpose because, being cold formed, it doesn't have the same characteristics in that it doesn't retain the proportions between the materials. In addition, it can lead to problems of separation between the layers. Separation can allow air – and other fluids – to enter between the layers which can lead to corrosion. Delamination is, of course, especially likely in components which vibrate regularly. The other problem is compression where the material is bent or distorted in some other way; the layer of adhesive can become compressed and degrade the characteristics of the material."

persuade prospects to consider
one or more other differentiators as
more important than price

predominant in prospects' minds. The typical example is price, where your product is the most, or one of the most, expensive alternatives. The task, then, is to persuade prospects to consider one or more other differentiators as more important than price. An example here comes from a drinking water treatment plant.

Continuous sand filters save costs and labor in drinking water plants

Water utilities are under pressure to keep costs under control and make the most efficient use of capital. These pressures are contributing to Waterlink's continuously operating sand filter, DynaSand, becoming standard equipment in Scandinavian water treatment plants. An example is a plant which invested in DynaSand filters when it underwent a major rebuild. It now operates, problem free, with only two staff.

When planning the rebuild, the operations manager recalls that there was really only one alternative option to the DynaSand filters: "this was that we ourselves build lamella-type sedimentation systems in the existing sedimentation tanks. The problems with this plan was that manual cleaning of the plates would have been necessary and would have taken about half a day. The existing tanks had to be cleaned out monthly and took about the same time so there would have been no labor saving. In addition, the actual building of the lamella system would have unavoidably disturbed the operation of the plant for several months at least. Running costs would also have been higher because the consumption of precipitation chemicals in the DynaSand units is about 40% lower compared with the alternative technique."

Despite being more expensive, Waterlink's DynaSand equipment won on two counts; firstly, manual cleaning is not necessary and secondly,

> the DynaSand units could be built beside the old plant while it contin-
> ued to operate. The switch-over to the new system was carried out
> within an hour or so and supply to the consumers was not interrupted.
>
> DynaSand is known in the US under the name "Supersand Continuous
> Sand Filter."

The self-build alternative would definitely have cost less initially, but the operating costs (in terms of labor and chemicals) and the disruption of supply eventually
out-weighed this short-term consideration.

Redefining

Redefining involves encouraging prospects to reconceptualize the "product package"
in question. This can be necessary where, for example, your product category is conventionally seen as a commodity, as in this example concerning conveyor belt systems.

Conveyor systems – problems and what can be done about them

> Most conveyor belt maintenance activities and replacements are nec-
> essary because of mechanical damage, not wear. This article looks at
> system components, ways to avoid mechanical damage, reduce down-
> time, and extend belt life. The Swedish-based, global mining and
> construction equipment group, Svedala, can provide both the advice
> and the integrated conveyor technology necessary to achieve this. The
> president of Svedala's conveying division, says: "conveying systems are,
> in fact, rather complicated".
>
> Unfortunately, many buyers tend to see them as simple and to buy
> their components as commodities especially the belt. In the majority of
> cases, belt replacement is required not because of wear but as a result
> of mechanical damage. He goes on to identify the causes of such
> damage and suggests solutions.

Typical problems in conveyor systems and suggested solutions

Belt slippage There are three main reasons why belt to pulley slippage occurs. The coefficient of friction between the belt and the pulley might be too low. The angle of wrap can be too small or the pre-tensioning of the belt is too low. The most cost efficient solution to a slippage problem is to increase the coefficient or friction by using pulley lagging. With the right design the pulley lagging will also prevent build up of transported material and snow and ice on the pulley.

Material adhering to the belt Sticky material can adhere to the belt, or dry material can get stuck in wear cavities on the belt. When the belt is running, material can fall off, building up on or under the conveyor. It can also cause damage to the underside of the belt and idlers. The splice is usually the first to fail. This problem was originally solved by manual maintenance and the installation of a timber scraper. However, if the cause of the problem is sticky material, the answer can be Svedala's two-scraper system.

Side spillage at loading stations Material tends to tumble and bounce when dropping onto a conveyor belt particularly if the transfer point is at a 90 degree angle to the receiving conveyor. Combined with the fact that the use of idlers leads to sagging of the belt between them, this may lead to spillage of material over the side of the conveyor belt in the transfer area. This problem can easily be solved by installing a Svedala loading station combined with a Svedala sealing system. The impact bars prevent sagging of the belt and the low friction top cover offers a flat surface for the sealing blocks to seal against.

Impact damage to the belt Especially prevalent where it carries very coarse or sharp-edged materials that cause weak points, holes, or even tears in the belt. In some occurrences the full length of the belt may be slit. Steel cord belt without rip-protection is especially vulnerable to this sort of slitting. The answer to the problems above is to use a Svedala loading station. The composite impact bars consisting of an aluminium track for fastening, special rubber for impact absorption and a low-friction, top-surface of UHD-PE prevent damage to the belt.

Mis-aligned belts Mis-tracking belts cause major costs. Svedala belt guiding systems can cut maintenance costs substantially through actively controlling and guiding the belt back on the right track. Moreover, revenues increase as a result of higher conveying capacity due to reduced material spillage. The risk of costly, unscheduled maintenance shutdowns due to belt damage can also be reduced considerably by installing Svedala belt guiding system, providing a maintenance-free solution. Unquestionably, a good working environment is important. Since material spillage is reduced with Svedala belt guiding system, a cleaner working environment is obtained. In addition, the cost for continuous cleaning of the work site can be minimized.

The argument presented here is that it is a wide-spread mistake to regard the components of conveyor systems, especially belts, as commodities, and that production time and money can be saved, plus other benefits obtained, by obtaining expert advice from the global leader and purchasing better quality and more sophisticated equipment.

Trading-off

The trading-off strategy involves getting prospects to understand that there may be more desirable alternatives, in terms of cost-effectiveness or other criteria than their initial objective. The example here concerns a Danish local authority.

☀ The cost savings of converting small sewage plants to pump stations – a case from Denmark

A Danish local authority originally planned to up-grade one of its small treatment plants to comply with new environmental regulations. ITT Flygt suggested that it convert it to a pump station.

▶

> **Up-grading/conversion study**
>
> The local authority commission consultants to carry out a study of the relative costs of up-grading the existing plant versus converting it into a pump station. In their report the consultants estimated that up-grading the plant would cost the authority nearly twice as much as converting it to a pump station, which decided the question.
>
> The sewage is now pumped, via a new 6-kilometer sewage pipe to the authority's main treatment plant. There is a distinct trend in Denmark for water authorities to adopt this strategy, of closing smaller plants and pumping sewage to larger ones, in order to maximize the economies of scale in the treatment process.

By helping to convince them that this pump station conversion was in fact the superior option to treatment plant up-grading, ITT Flygt was able to sell this (and other) authorities their latest, state-of-the-art pump station package.

Resolving of concerns

The idea here is that even when a prospect is more or less convinced that they should purchase the product, they often have concerns about whether it's going to work as claimed by the vendor. Rackham emphasizes that resolving concerns is specific for each particular customer. However, as stressed in Chapter Two, the experience of the sales force will reveal (in this and other areas) trends and patterns which can be generalized into marcoms messages. As with the other marcoms task areas above, the most effective cases can be used to carry the appropriate message. The example here concerns insulation material for a deep-sea oil field.

The reliability of this insulation material is clearly crucial to the operators of such sub-sea oil fields. The rigorous comparative testing carried out by this purchaser should, however, reassure other prospects. Trelleborg's salespeople could give them a copy of this case story (ideally published in an off-shore journal with which the prospect is familiar) and encourage them to contact the purchaser (who's named in the original text) to confirm their test findings.

Rubber insulation for the frontiers of sub-sea oil production

"Hot Ice" can cause havoc in sub-sea pipework. The risk of its formation increases with the depth of an off-shore field. However, Trelleborg has now come up with an insulation material which, tests indicate, can provide effective protection down to 1,500 m.

The project engineer for a new, exceptionally deep, oil field off the African coast has had to solve the crucial problem of cold oil due to the wellhead depth. "This varies," he explains, "from about 1,150 to 1,450 m, which compares with North Sea and other offshore fields which usually have depths of between 300 and 500 m. In the North Sea, oil emerges at a temperature of about 110°C whereas, because of this field's water depth, the oil temperature is only 65°C. If the temperature of the oil goes down to around 22°C 'hot ice' or hydrate formations can occur: water and gas is mixed in with the oil, possibly forming solid plugs. These can block the pipes and are enormously difficult to get rid of. Counter measures, such as heating the pipes or depressurizing them or adding methanol in order to lower the freezing point, are likely to take six to eight weeks to have an effect. In addition, 'hot ice' is really quite dangerous. Pipes can burst or even explode and plugs of hot ice can emerge from broken pipes like cannonballs causing serious damage and injury to people."

Testing insulation

Insulating the pipes was an alternative and extensive tests of insulation materials were carried out. "We looked at about 12 different types of materials and rigorously tested six of these," the project engineer recalls. "Among these were various types of polyurethane and epoxy-based materials and also some other manufacturers offering rubber solutions although Trelleborg was the only vulcanized material considered." The materials were tested under conditions simulating both service depth and service life. This was done by accelerated time test;

for example, materials were kept at 200 bar for seven weeks and at an elevated temperature of 93°C. This represents 21 years at 20°C at the actual pressure at the sub-sea system, which is 150 bar.

Why Trelleborg was chosen

"There are three main benefits of the Trelleborg material," the project engineer explains. "It gives very good corrosion protection, has excellent resistance to deterioration in dark, wet environments such as the sea bed and is pliable so that when the pipes flex with temperature and pressure variations, there is no cracking of the insulation material."

SUMMARY: CASES AS STRATEGIC SALES TOOLS

All the editorial examples presented in this chapter can (and probably have) been used in this way – first published in a relevant trade journal to gain immediate readership – but more importantly to acquire a stamp of published editorial legitimacy. Once this has been obtained, copies of the published version can be assigned to the armory of the sales force for use at appropriate moments in the sales process. On the issue of copyright: the text belongs to the author and pictures belong to the photographer or illustrator. A company should first ensure that it has the permission of these people to use the material as it wishes. It's true that the copyright to the *format* published by the journal belongs to that journal. However, this is unlikely to constrain a company's use of published editorial material because, firstly, the material is supplied free of charge to the journal by the company (our agency, for example, always includes a statement reserving the right to use the published format as conditional on the free supply of the material) and, secondly, it's highly unlikely

first published to acquire legitimacy

then assigned to the sales force

for use in the sales process

that a journal would want to alienate a company that supplies it with editorial material and is probably also a potential advertiser.

In practical terms, the optimal way to make published articles available to a company's global sales force is to first scan them and then store them in a database on the company's intranet. Salespeople anywhere in the world can then search the database by product, applications, etc. looking for exactly the article they need for the particular prospect they're about to visit. E-business technology now allows this to be done, on a global scale, relatively easily.

NOTE

1. Downes, L. and Mui, C. (1998) *Killer applications.* Boston, MA: Harvard Business Press.

chapter eight

E-BUSINESS

FOR B2B

Worldwide there are currently 300 million internet users – this is estimated to rise to 1 billion by 2005. This chapter looks at several examples of how B2B companies are making use of the new possibilities opened up by the internet. To continue a theme of this book, we can begin by highlighting the differences between B2B and B2C in this area. From a B2C perspective, it's clear that, around the end of the 1990s, there was a surge of enthusiasm for e-commerce. After a number of years, the so-called dot com bubble burst, leaving in its wake significant disillusionment with the internet as a business tool among investors and other interested parties. Away from the glare of media attention, some B2B companies (many of them from the so-called "old economy") have been busy learning how to use e-business to improve their operations.

At this point, I should clarify the terminology I'm using. "E-commerce" here means using the internet as a sales channel, i.e. conducting transactions with customers via a website instead of using the old channels, such as a personal sales force or bricks and mortar outlets. E-business, on the other hand, encompasses e-commerce but also includes all the other uses which economic organizations can make of the internet, such as: managing their own procurement and supply chains; building and maintaining long-term relationships with their key customers and intra-organizational information management. In these terms, we can say that the B2C.com start-ups, who were responsible for the bubble, were predominantly engaging in e-commerce, while the B2B pioneers are interested in implementing the whole range of e-business possibilities.

a major factor in the bursting

of the dot com bubble

was poor business practice

E-COMMERCE: A TRIUMPH OF HYPE OVER REALITY.COM?

Distinctions of this sort were illustrated, for example, in a debate, held in March 2001, at Cambridge University Union on the motion "E-commerce is a triumph of hype over reality.com". The general consensus which emerged from the debate was that a major factor in the bursting of the dot com bubble was poor business practice. Andrew Scott, a web consultant and owner of worldwidecity.com (which has worked on web solutions for companies such as Deutsche Bank, Freeserve and *The Economist*) claimed that, "most internet failures are due to bad management and poor marketing planning. E-commerce can be more than just a transaction achieved electronically – it provides technological opportunities for relationship building. The internet can be a complement to other channels, it doesn't have to compete with them. B2B is mainly using the internet for procurement." Nicola Horlick, Managing Director, SG Asset Management (a manager of major investment funds), commented that, "B2B companies have generally been more successful at e-business because they've incorporated it into already well-established and competent businesses."

E-commerce

provides technological opportunities

for relationship building

The efficiency dividend

Phil Smith, Director of Business Development for Cisco UK, emphasized the cost-cutting potentials, "E-business can reduce the operating expenses of companies by 20% or more. It does this by streamlining and automating bureaucratic tasks and eliminating a lot of the paperwork, which, of course, increases productivity. Eighty seven percent of CEOs are still planning to invest in e-business. Jack Walsh of GE reports that by implementing e-business, his company has been able to cut costs by $6–7 billion and Cisco, which has a turnover of $20 billion, has saved $1.3 billion in the same way. Ninety percent of Cisco's turnover comes through internet transactions. By using the internet, we are able to handle ten times the volume of business and with 25% higher customer satisfaction. By 2001, the British government is planning to handle 90% of its low-value transactions via the internet. Using the internet can cut the cost of procurement by 80%."

Just another tool

Another consensual conclusion from the debate was that, rather than representing some magic new world, the internet is just another tool like the telephone and the mail-order catalogue which technological development has put at the disposal of business people. Phil Smith commented that, "it's still surely *possible* to do business without using the telephone – but does anyone today *want* to do business without it?" A speaker from the floor pointed out that when the mail-order catalogue appeared in America about 100 years ago, it elicited the same predictions about the demise of "bricks and mortar" shopping. No doubt in a similar way, the use of the internet will further expand into the business world until it has taken over those functions for which it is the most efficient tool available. However rapid this development might be, it's still an evolution rather than a revolution.

CASE ILLUSTRATIONS: "OLD ECONOMY" INNOVATORS

We're now going to look at four examples of B2B companies that are entering the e-business world. As suggested above, in addition to e-commerce, B2B companies are using the internet for three other main functions; procurement, managing customer relationships, and intra-organizational information management. The first case, from Sandvik Steel, addresses most of these issues. Indeed, they are planning for levels of electronic integration between supply, producer, and customer at which the boundaries between three distinct organizations become highly problematic. The second case, from a small, entrepreneurial tool maker in California, illustrates a niche role for e-commerce in B2B. In Chapter Five it was suggested that e-commerce would tend to be the channel for B2B products which are perceived as commodities. An exception to this can be more significant products where use of the internet can significantly reduce transaction costs, as is the case with the purpose-designed cutting tools in case two. In case three, the metal-powder company Höganäs, illustrates a special aspect of the customer relations function – how consultancy services can be provided via an extranet. In the fourth case ITT Industries' Director of E-business describes how this large, diverse, and global group is taking advantage of e-business.

CASE ONE: SANDVIK STEEL

Sandvik Steel is one of the world's leading producers of tube, strip, wire, and bar products. It's part of the Sandvik Group and, like them, its headquarters are located in Sandviken, in central Sweden. All of Sandvik Steel's products are made from stainless steel and special alloys. The company concentrates on niche business areas, in which it is a world leader. It can also claim to be a pioneer among B2B companies in the implementation of e-business solutions.

"In most conventional, commercial organizations there's often a tension between 'user needs' and 'supplier needs,'" says Göran Nyström, vice president for sales and marketing at Sandvik Steel. "The production and sales administrative functions tend to focus on supplier needs, in other words, they are generally product-oriented, while marketing and product research concentrate on user needs, i.e. they're application-oriented." Göran sees the organizational transformations made possible by e-business as a means of integrating these divergent orientations and making the whole organization more outward-looking and application-focussed – in short, more case-based.

"Our objectives in e-business can be summarized as follows and roughly in this order:

- to improve the efficiency of our operations

- to enhance our capacity to build relationships with our customers

- to achieve "electronic integration" with our key customers.

With regard to the first point, Göran comments, "Just as with the introduction of previous communications technologies, such as the telephone, the basic idea behind the drive to adopt the internet as a channel is to make it easier to do business – and, just like the previous technologies, those who adopt it first and utilize it most effectively will have a competitive advantage."

Key-customer extranet

One of the main tools for achieving objectives two and three is the company's extranet, which was introduced in 1999. "Our extranet system is designed for our 'key customers'," explains Annika Roos, marketing manager at Sandvik Steel. "Each of these is given their own site in the system which they access via the ID codes we give them." How is "key customer" defined? "As with many other questions, e-business is forcing us to be much more precise about such definitions," says Annika. Generally speaking, the company uses three criteria:

- large volume of business
- high profitability for us
- large potential.

The actual selection of who counts as a key customer is left entirely to the national sales companies and product units (certain products and customers are assigned to global product units) and they remain very much "their" customers. "This is an important point because we're trying very hard not to alienate our sales companies around the world during this process of transition to e-business. For reasons of language and culture and also because personal relationships are always going to be crucial in B2B transactions, our policy is to integrate our sales companies into our e-business development. Once selected, the local company or product unit will invite the customer to join our extranet and will make presentations to them regarding the advantages of doing so," says Annika.

Menu of services

"We have a menu of services which are available via our extranet. This includes: e-commerce, a special online customer magazine, technical training materials, catalogues, technical data, and an intra-company communications system. Another choice for the sales companies is which of these service options to offer each particular customer. A basic issue here is the strength of the relationship we have with that particular customer: a lot of the services we're making available in this way give access to the knowledge base which is one of our main competitive advantages. We certainly don't want to give away this knowledge to our competitors. Consequently, there has to be a fairly high level of trust between us and the customers to whom we offer our full extranet service. There are also other criteria for tailoring the service to particular customers, e.g. larger customers may have their own purchasing system and therefore wouldn't be interested in our e-commerce option." Once the customer's extranet site is set up, it's up to them and "their" Sandvik sales company how they want to develop it.

"Our current goal," Annika explains, "is to have 200 'actively functioning' sites by the middle of this year (2001), and we're running an internal project called 'extra push' to encourage this." In total, about 400 customer sites have been set up, so far. But how do Sandvik Steel define an "actively functioning" site? Göran Nyström replies that, "Pre-e-business, communication between us and a customer's organization flowed pretty exclusively through the relevant salesperson in our organization to the relevant purchaser in theirs. Now we're opening up a much wider person-to-person interface between the two organizations. For example, individuals in the production or R&D departments of each organization can now communicate directly with each other. With our most advanced customer extranet sites we're approaching the point where the interface more or less ceases to exist – we're sharing large parts of our internal information systems. The ultimate would be a seamless merging of the two systems. This can start with sharing basic information like stock levels and can expand into areas like product development and R&D. Our aim is to 'lock in' customers by providing superior value. Part of this involves making the information flow between our two organizations as easy and extensive as possible." (See Figure 8.1.)

we're opening up
a much wider person-to-person interface

between the two organizations

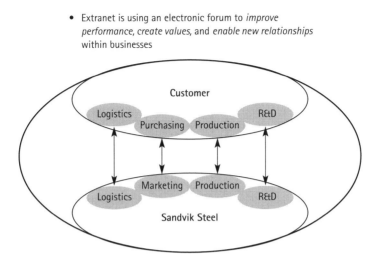

- Extranet is using an electronic forum to *improve performance, create values,* and *enable new relationships* within businesses

Figure 8.1 What is extranet?

Certificate archive

Annika Roos adds that, "test certificates are a practical example of what we're currently using the customer sites for: these documents certify the agreed specification for the material we supply, including chemical composition, ISO standards, etc. Such certificates can be important for our customers, for example, in a situation where their customer required them to trace back the original composition of the materials they used. Previously, these were packed with the material when shipped from our plants and possibly also posted or faxed ahead to the customer. Now we post the relevant certificates on the customer's extranet site. This means, firstly, that they have instant access to them 24/7 and, perhaps more importantly, we undertake to archive them for at least ten years on the site, so, in effect, we're taking over the archive function in this area for them."

Göran points out that some of the barriers to progress in this area are still technological: "We've already achieved some progress on the integration front; orders corresponding to 10% of our invoicing value are now transmitted directly computer-to-computer. The major constraint in the EDI (electronic data interchange) area is a lack of universal standards. There's EDIFACT, which was developed by the UN 20 years ago, though this still requires translators at either end and is rather basic. XML (extended mark-up language) is more sophisticated but, as yet, lacks universal standards."

we need to escape from
the "culture of secrecy"
in which possessing and concealing
knowledge is used as a power base

Changing the organizational culture

The major obstacles to this sort of inter-organization integration, however, are in the realm of organizational culture. Göran says, "We need to change from a culture of 'sending and receiving' to one of 'depositing and searching'. We have to change our attitudes to information: we need to escape from the 'culture of secrecy' in which possessing and concealing knowledge is used as a power base. Instead we have to reward and promote people who openly share, spread, and develop knowledge. Inevitably though, changing cultures is a gradual process."

Annika Roos adds, "a lot of the effort of becoming 'an e-business' involves overcoming resistance and fear within your own organization: you need to change people's patterns of thinking and reacting. We've found that a lot of resistance comes from the 'now-I've-got-to-do-this-too!' reaction," i.e. instead of seeing the potential for making their jobs easier and more interesting, many people see the conversion to e-business as just another burdensome task. A lot of the fear is, of course, connected with job security: "if we make our product databases directly accessible to our customers, our people, who previously used them to provide information to customers by 'phone, start asking themselves 'what's going to be left for me to do?' The constructive answer is that instead of providing the "mechanical details" of products, which customers can now find for themselves, the displaced people can be assigned to investigating and answering more subtle and open-ended questions about product characteristics. For the transition process to be successful, it's important that people in the organization see their colleagues being assigned to other (hopefully more stimulating) tasks when their previous jobs get automated away by e-business."

e-business isn't a specialist area of the business, it's the whole organization in an electronic environment

Avoid specialists

An important part of this new flexibility of roles, involves getting everyone to take responsibility for e-business activities – e-business isn't a specialist area of the business, it's the whole organization in an electronic environment. Annika comments, "in connection with establishing our customer extranet, the sales companies were obliged to make someone responsible for setting up and managing customer sites. Almost invariably, their IT manager was selected for this task. We learned that this generally meant that very little was going to happen, the problem being that the IT manager may not know very much about the company's customers or its sales and marketing operations. Ideally, someone from sales and marketing should be responsible for this area, so now we require every company to appoint both a commercial and an IT "champion." The commercial champion's job is to explain, both to customers and to the company's own sales force, how an extranet customer site can be developed for the mutual benefit of their organization and ours. The point here is that, from a business point of view, our customer extranet is not part of our IT system – it's now our most important sales and marketing tool and consequently should be managed as such. A basic principle is that whoever is responsible for a particular area within our organization, should also be responsible for handling this area in our e-business environment: e-business is not something that can be delegated to our IT people."

Technoculture vs infoculture

Göran Nyström says, "It's also very important *how* you get people to adapt to e-business. I like to talk, in this context, about a 'tale of two cultures'; technoculture and infoculture (see Figure 8.2). The technoculture approach is to dictate, from the

"evolution" not
revolution

top down, how the organization's e-business systems are to be designed and built. As we've mentioned already, the problem with this approach is that it generates fear, resistance, or indifference. The best way to get people to actually use and develop e-business systems is to let them do it themselves – 'evolution' not 'revolution'. This way you can literally 'grow' e-business through the co-operation of everyone involved."

Technoculture
- Reductionist
- Architectural
- Machine-centered
- Revolutionary

Infoculture
- Holistic
- Ecological
- Human-centered
- Evolutionary

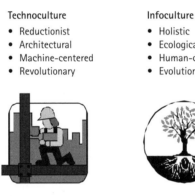

Figure 8.2 A tale of two cultures

CASE TWO: INTERNET ORDERING FOR CUTTING TOOLS

Through an interactive, internet process, buyers of rotary cutting tools can now receive a complete quotation within 45–60 seconds and at 40%–60% less cost than conventional ordering. In addition, all tools ordered from the site are customized – potentially making the standard tool obsolete.

David Povich, president of Tool Alliance, of Huntington Beach, California, explains the process by which cutting tools are conventionally specified and ordered. "First a requisition will be sent to an internal buyer during the tooling-up phase for a new manufacturing operation. The buyer will then contact tool manufacturers via either their salespeople or their distributors. The tool manufacturers will then produce quotes which will be sent back the same route, and finally the manufacturer makes a choice of which toolmaker to buy from. This process might take anything from five to ten days."

Standardized style options

Tungsten Toolworks, a division of Tool Alliance, has now set up a site, http://www.tungstentoolworks.com, where this entire process has been reduced to between 45 seconds to 1 minute. The first step for a potential customer coming to the site is to give a name and address and receive a password. Next he is presented with 12 different style alternatives for the tool he is looking for. Tungsten Toolworks have standardized style options into these alternatives. They appear on the site and are shown as easy-to-recognize shaded drawings with instructions accompanying each, as to types of application and materials for which they are suitable. The customer simply clicks on the style of tool with which he wishes to proceed. The next step for the customer is to specify the dimensions of the tool he requires. Since this is a website, and consequently globally accessible, the dimensions can be specified in either metric or imperial values. Also at this stage, the customer can order other features such as coatings if required and if so, of which type. He can also select between options regarding the quantity of units he wishes to purchase.

45 seconds for a quote

Having entered this data the customer will be presented with a drawing of the tool, including dimensions which he has now specified. On the same page, prices are given for the three quantity options specified by the customer together with estimated delivery times. The complete quotation including the drawing can also be e-mailed to the customer for confirmation.

This is the first website, as far as David Povich knows, that can offer such a system for specifying and ordering customized cutting tools. He claims that, "the system of on-site specifications and ordering of cutting tools has the potential to revolutionize this business in terms of price and delivery times." Using this system, Tungsten Toolworks have been able to reduce their costs of quoting by 50%.

Prices reduced by 40% to 60%

"This means that we can offer tools from the site at prices that are 40% to 60% below those available through conventional specification and ordering systems. In addition our costs for the process are now more fair and transparent: when we quote from the site, customers are charged strictly in proportion to the amount of grinding involved in the tool they require. Traditionally, especially for standard tools, pricing has tended not to be calculated according to the amount of grinding involved in the production. In other words, customers from our site will now be paying only for what they are actually getting. We are also delivering the tools on the average 50% faster than the estimated times quoted on the site, and generally this process is 25% to 90% faster than the conventional buying process."

The role for distributors

As to the site's global reach, Povich reports that they received orders from, for example, the UK and Hong Kong, which they were able to deliver within four to five days. Invoicing and delivery for orders from the site are handled by the company's existing distributor network. Povich says that, "keeping our distributors onboard during the process of developing the site has been a key element in our strategy. We believe that distributors will still have a vital role in our business, especially in terms of the personal relationships with which they are able to support our customers. Therefore we have kept them fully informed and involved during the whole process of developing our site."

Customized as standard

One development for the future which Povich believes his site could well bring about is to transform the division in the cutting tool business between standard and customized tools. "What you can say about our site is that – in effect – we are making customized tools standard." The division in the industry at present is that customized tools represent between 40% and 50% of the market, but Povich points out that they are not very profitable for the toolmakers. "Customized tools currently represent only about 15% of Ultra Tool's business. On the other hand, we fully expect the Tungsten Toolworks site to be our fastest growing division for the future, and this site is of course exclusively supplying customized tools. It is simply that the traditional way of quoting for and producing customized tools was expensive. For manufacturers customized tools are clearly an advantage, because they can be specifically designed for the application in which they're needed. Generally speaking, customized tools – if purchased in a reasonable quantity – will currently cost approximately three times as much as an equivalent standard tool. Consequently, customers often buy standard tools and attempt themselves to adapt them to their particular application, which is nearly always sub-optimal, compared with having a tool customized in the first place."

CASE THREE: HÖGANÄS – B2B CONSULTANCY VIA AN EXTRANET

A Swedish-based, world leader in the metal powder business is developing problem-solving, extranet consultancy services, including high-resolution video, for its key customers.

Höganäs, has been in the metal powders business for over 100 years and is a well-established world leader in this business. This makes it well placed to ride the tidal wave of sintered part technology which is just beginning to surge through the global automotive industry. Höganäs is the largest producer of metal powders in the world, both by volume and turnover. It is also the largest specialist and independent producer of metal powders: it has three major global competitors, two in North America and one in Japan, but these are large industrial groups which are also involved in many other branches of industry. Höganäs produces between 8 and 20 basic metal powder products and these represent about 50% of their sales. The remaining 50% are mixes of these basic powders, and possibly other materials, specific to particular customer applications.

Application areas

These products are predominantly used in six application areas: the biggest (68%) is the supply of material for sintered parts, mainly for the automotive industry. Second (10%) is the use of "sponge iron" (Höganäs's original metal powder product) as an aid to welding. "Thermal surfacing" where the metal powders are used as components in coating represents about 6% of Höganäs's business. SMCs (Soft Magnetic Composites) can be used for the manufacture of electric motors. This currently represents about 3% of sales but has considerable potential for future growth.

"Carrier cores" are materials used in the toner for copying machines and printers. This application started in the late 1970s and now represents about 1% of sales. Most of the remainder (around 8%) goes to the chemical and metallurgical industries for various applications such as additives in pharmaceuticals, components, food and animal feeds, and plastics and other metals products. Out of all these application areas the automotive industry is clearly the most important in strategic terms: "Our goal is to become the clearly predominate global supplier of raw material for sintered parts in the automotive business," states Hans Söderhjelm, Höganäs AB's marketing manager.

Partnerships for material development

Hans Söderhjelm, explains the steps which Höganäs follows in its projects to produce the material for a new sintered part. "These are very long-term projects and can last from one to six years. At the beginning we get presented with a part which is currently being manufactured by traditional methods, either forged or – more generally these days – machined. The task then is to produce exactly the same part by the sintered technique – obviously we start with its existing specification."

The steps in the project then run as follows:

- Höganäs develop a material suitable for the part. (This might take up to a year and a half.)
- the material is tested, both by Höganäs and by the customer. (This can take 10 months.)
- the material has to achieve a whole series of approvals, including the internal approvals at Höganäs and by the automotive manufacturer and in addition approval under national and international standards. This can take six months and also involves assessing the commercial viability of the material
- the next step is to look at the production process and how the material performs in this context
- there is a quality control stage, when for example the part is being used in prototype vehicles.

Extranet services

Höganäs has recently introduced a number of customer information services to further enhance the quality of its service. In 1998, they set up their own extranet known as HIPIH which stands for Höganäs Iron Powder Information Hub. HIPIH is available to selected key customers, who have to apply to get access to it via a user password. HIPIH contains the following features:

- A "webalog" containing detailed product specifications and performance characteristics of the various materials (which are not available elsewhere)

- Health and safety data

- Product statistical data – processes, properties, etc. (ISO 9001)

- Powder metal school

- Quality

- Metallography

- Machinability

- Warm compaction

} Pedagogic texts
(available in various languages)

- Published articles – conference and technical papers published by Höganäs people and others going back to the 1970s

- "*Powder News*" – an online version of the Höganäs in-house magazine

- Commodity prices – these are the prices of Höganäs's raw materials. This provides a form of open book keeping to give customers information regarding the basis on which the prices they pay (which are generally unique to each customer) are calculated

- Vehicle statistics – worldwide statistics on the automotive industry

- Customer service investigations – see below

- Computer aided selection of iron powder – this system, unique to Höganäs, enables customers to select precisely which type of metal powder product is suitable for their particular application

- Complaints

- E-meeting – video conferencing facility

- E-commerce – mainly available for the reordering of pre-established regular supplies by those customers who want to use this channel. It can also be used for ordering materials, making payments, checking delivery times, etc.

Customer service investigations

CSI is a highly innovative feature of HIPIH. Hans Söderhjelm explains that, "our idea with this is to 'computerize' our system for handling the customer-initiated investigations which we receive. It often happens that customers will want to use our material in ways which they hadn't fully anticipated when they ordered it, for example, the temperatures at which the material should be sintered, questions about its properties, e.g. the material may change color at certain temperatures, and various other technical issues around the metal powder product."

Höganäs's old way of handling such issues proceeded as follows: the customer would contact the company's local representative with the question. He or she would then have to arrange for a sample of the material and/or part to be couriered back to Höganäs's head office in Sweden. The specialists at head office would then examine the sample and produce a report which addressed the customer's question. This report would be sent to the local representative, who would then present it to the customer. This entire process could take anything from two weeks to two months.

"Internet-CSI", however, is a lot faster. The initial customer enquiry can now go direct to the head-office specialists via e-mail from the website, and the samples, rather than having to be physically transported around the world, can now be examined by high-resolution video. Customers and Höganäs specialists can view metal samples together, via video, across the world. Hans comments that, "this is basically the same technique used in 'remote medicine', where a doctor can examine a patient and even carry out surgery via high-resolution video. One of the problems we face in implementing this technique at present is the lack of the necessary broadband communications infrastructure in various parts of the world. Another major issue is training for our customers, both in using this sort of communications technology and in a sufficiently high-level of metallurgical knowledge to make this remote problem solving work. Our large customers, who have enormous, often multi-national organizations, already have these levels of competence, but this is generally not the case for our small and medium-sized customers."

Formal customer training

To address this last problem, Höganäs offers, as part of its cost-free, after-sales service, considerable formal training to customers' personnel. Its PM (Powder

Metal) school was started in 1990. "Generally speaking each customer will send a production engineer to participate in one of these one-week courses. They deal with the whole theory of sintered parts, both the materials required and the production processes involved. These courses can be taught in any language and in more or less any location around the world," says Hans. More recently, Höganäs has started courses in metalography, which is the science of diagnosing the condition of metals from images of their surfaces, usually highly magnified. This again is offered cost-free to customers. The metalography school is especially relevant to Höganäs's high-resolution video conferencing service.

"These training and diagnostic services are unique to Höganäs and significantly differentiate us from our competitors," claims Hans. "Because of the nature of our business, there is no actual direct selling of products via the internet – in the sense of making a first contact with a new customer via this channel. As a B2B materials specialist, our approach has been to use the internet for 'remote consultancy'. A further step in this direction, which we're planning, is to make our own knowledge database, or metal powder expert system, available, via our extranet, to our key customers. People will be able to search this either by looking at the actual questions which customers have previously asked us to investigate or by searching on topics such as: temperature, color, tensile strength, impact energy, etc. Again, this will have a higher utility for our small and medium-sized customers – the larger ones have such systems of their own. A system like this will enable customers themselves to find the solution to 90% of the problems which they currently bring to our attention. This gives us the opportunity to concentrate on the 10% where we have to carry out additional research to find the solution. This doesn't, however, mean that we'll lose the problem-solving relationship with 90% of our customers: we can obviously monitor who accesses our database and what issues they're looking at. This gives us the opportunity to intervene in person if we think we can provide additional help or to follow up the implementation of solutions, etc."

 CASE FOUR: ITT INDUSTRIES

Mark Goetze, ITT Industries' Director of E-business was 30 when appointed to this job. "That may seem young," he comments, "but I've got 12 years' experience of business technology and five years' of the internet. I'm a grizzled veteran by web standards." When asked, "what is 'e-business'?" Goetze replies, "the goal of e-busi-

"the goal of e-business

is to move your business information and internal processes

into an electronic format using internet-based technologies

ness is to move your business information and internal processes into an electronic format using internet-based technologies. Instant access to information is key; get your computer systems talking to each other internally and talking to your suppliers and customers externally. Instead of human beings making phone calls or manually moving lots of paper from Point A to Point B, we're going to let the computers do it. In the old-world economy we were known as a bricks and mortar company: our goal is to become a clicks and mortar enterprise. ITT Industries had been introducing e-business projects at the level of the individual companies in the Group for years but the real 'birth' of e-business as a corporate initiative happened in March 2000. Travis Engen, our Chairman and CEO, formally introduced it as one of four major growth initiatives at an executive conference. From that point on, we had an organization that understood the importance of e-business both as a top priority of our CEO and as critical to the future success of ITT Industries."

So, having announced its intention to become an e-business, what exactly is the company doing differently? ITT Industries has targeted three main areas for e-change.

Purchasing (e-procurement)

With e-procurement, the Group is automating the purchasing process for enterprise-wide, operational items like paper, computers, and office furniture. Items like these will be purchased online from a centralized database. Suppliers will post their catalogue (or "webalog") on a secure internet site which can be accessed by ITT Industries' users. Purchasing managers who need pens, for example, will visit the site, choose a pen and type in their order. All orders will be compiled in a master database, and order transmission and tracking will be handled online. Anyone in the Group who's involved in purchasing supplies and services will receive web-based training. Centralizing procurement, via the web, should significantly reduce the cost of procuring supplies and services and improve productivity in order placement and invoice processing.

Supply chain management

On the supply chain side, ITT Industries is working with several global services companies to create applications that will automate and optimize each value center's supply chain. Goetze explains, "when somebody in operations orders a part, there will be an electronic communication to the ordering system. The system will dispatch the part and 'bundle' orders for the supplier. With no paper pushing, the part arrives faster and time-to-market decreases. And by buying in bulk, we can often gain cost advantages."

Online order management

The third initiative is online order management capability. Several of the value centers within fluid technology and cannon are developing web-based tools which link directly to their ERP systems; allowing OEM's and distributors to submit and track orders via the web. Giving our customers the capability to enter, update, and track their purchase orders online automates a very manpower-intensive function and ultimately improves customer satisfaction.

Implementation

The complexity of ITT Industries as an organization has made e-business implementation less than straightforward: "we are global – many different marketplaces with many different products. We want to attack this at an enterprise-wide level, but many of the battles will have to be won at the value center level first. For example, we'll try an e-business idea in one division in one country first, then migrate it to that division worldwide and then perhaps across other divisions of ITT Industries. To regulate this progression, we've established a 90-day rule. If a local e-business team implements a plan or an idea, they have to show results in 90 days. Are people using it? Does it provide a benefit to our business? Is it decreasing costs or increasing revenue? If the answers are yes, we'll take the idea to the next level."

"The areas of ITT Industries that are furthest ahead are generally, those that do business with other e-businesses. A perfect example is our connectors business. They do business with Motorola, Siemens, and Nokia – companies that have nudged and pushed their suppliers in this direction. And our pumps business has

Today's world is a web world and

to succeed in it we need

to move at e-speed

been effective in centralizing their e-business efforts, which helps accelerate the process. In many of the markets we serve we are on par with our competitors, but they are not an ideal benchmark. We want to raise the bar and compare ourselves with e-business leaders like Honeywell, General Electric, and IBM. We have a chance to set the pace for our industry. Because we are a leader in many of our markets, we get approached very often by customers and suppliers who want to partner with us. We need to take advantage of that opportunity."

E-business benefits?

"E-business will allow us to access new marketplaces, reach new customers, and because we're operating 24/7, it will accelerate our revenue stream. We'll save costs by automating processes. If we're getting products to market faster and making it easier to order from us, customer satisfaction will go up. And without a lot of manual work-arounds, we'll improve employee productivity and job satisfaction. In the end, our goal is to become the premier global products and services company through the use of e-business applications. Today's world is a web world and to succeed in it we need to move at e-speed."

SUMMARY: ANOTHER TOOL FOR COMPETENT B2B BUSINESSES

These B2B companies (from the "old economy") are forging ahead into the e-business world. As noted above, they've generally been more successful at this because they've incorporated e-business into already well-established and competent businesses. They're finding that the internet is just another tool which technological development has put at their disposal. Its use will expand within their businesses until it has taken over those functions for which it is the most efficient tool available.

B2B MARKETING

216

Index

INDEX

INDEX

223

More power to your [business-mind]

Even at the end there's more we can learn. More that *we* can learn from your experience of this book, and more ways to add to *your* learning experience.

For who to read, what to know and where to go in the world of business, visit us at **business-minds.com**.

Here you can find out more about the people and ideas that can make you and your business more innovative and productive. Each month our e-newsletter, *Business-minds Express*, delivers an infusion of thought leadership, guru interviews, new business practice and reviews of key business resources directly to you. Subscribe for free at

▶ **www.business-minds.com/goto/newsletters**

Here you can also connect with ways of putting these ideas to work. Spreading knowledge is a great way to improve performance and enhance business relationships. If you found this book useful, then so might your colleagues or customers. If you would like to explore corporate purchases or custom editions personalised with your brand or message, then just get in touch at

▶ **www.business-minds.com/corporatesales**

We're also keen to learn from your experience of our business books – so tell us what you think of this book and what's on *your* business mind with an online reader report at business-minds.com. Together with our authors, we'd like to hear more from you and explore new ways to help make these ideas work at

▶ **www.business-minds.com/goto/feedback**

[www.business-minds.com
www.financialminds.com]